TWO-WAY STREET

USA – EUROPE ARMS PROCUREMENT

The Klepsch Report
with a foreword by
The Rt. Hon. Geoffrey Rippon

BRASSEY'S · LONDON
CRANE RUSSAK · NEW YORK

© 1979 Brassey's Publishers Limited
Production by Youé and Spooner Limited
Published in the United Kingdom by
Brassey's Publishers Limited
10, Upper Berkeley Street
Portman Square
London, W1H 7PE
ISBN 0-904609-33-2

Published in the United States by
Crane, Russak & Company Inc.
347 Madison Avenue
New York, New York 10017
ISBN 0-8448-1374-5
LC 78-73557

Printed in Great Britain

Preface

History of The Klepsch Report

In recent years individual Members of the European Parliament have been voicing growing concern at the absence of cooperation in the defence equipment field. High and rising costs for Member States, increasing dependence on the U.S.A., inadequate investment in technological innovation and a resultant decline in Europe's competitive capability in the world, were among some of the many critical comments continually being voiced by Members. It was largely against this background that sufficient support was eventually raised for action to be taken by the European Parliament.

At its meeting of 18 January 1977, the Political Affairs Committee appointed Dr Egon KLEPSCH, a German member of the Parliament and Chairman of the Christian Democrat Group, as rapporteur. The Political Committee considered the Klepsch Report at four meetings in 1977 and 1978. On 21 April 1978 the Political Committee adopted the Klepsch Report and the draft resolution submitted by Egon Klepsch, which accompanied it, by 20 votes to 5 with 3 abstentions.

On 17 March 1977 the European Parliament's Committee on Economic and Monetary Affairs appointed Mr Tom NORMANTON, a British Conservative M.P., draftsman for its opinion. On 21 March 1978 the Committee adopted Tom NORMANTON's opinion unanimously, with one abstention.

On 13 June 1978 the European Parliament debated the Klepsch Report and the Normanton opinion, and on the following day adopted the resolution submitted to it by Egon Klepsch in a vote, taken by show of hands, by a convincing majority.

Speaking in the debate on 13 June 1978 the Vicomte DAVIGNON, the Commissioner responsible for industrial policy welcomed the Klepsch Report and the resolution on behalf of the Commission and promised that the Commission would make proposals along the lines set out in the Klepsch Report. The Commission's proposals are now awaited.

Dr Egon A. KLEPSCH M.d.B. is the Chairman of the Christian Democrat Group of the European Parliament. A University lecturer on international politics, he has since 1965 been Member of the German Bundestag for Koblenz. Since 1970 Dr Klepsch has been Member of the Parliamentary Assembly of the Council of Europe, WEU and the North Atlantic Assembly, and since 1973 Member of the European Parliament.

Tom Normanton, Conservative M.P. for Cheadle (1970) has been a Member of the European Parliament since January 1973 where he is a member of the European Conservative Group. He serves on the Parliament's Economic and Monetary Affairs Committee, and is Vice-Chairman of the Energy and Research Committee. Throughout his life he has been active in the field of industry, currently being President of the International Textiles Manufacturers Federation. In the European Parliament he concentrates on industrial policy matters, and as a former Staff Officer he takes a special interest in European defence.

Contents

Foreword by theRt. Hon. Geoffrey Rippon MP

The Klepsch Report

Part I: Political Aspects
1. Common Industrial Policy — 18
2. Attempts to achieve European procurement cooperation at the Atlantic level — 19
3. Some problems — 30
4. The US Challenge — 36
5. Collaborative Projects — 42
6. The Community and European Armaments Procurement — 45
7. Conclusions and Proposals — 48

Part II: The Industrial Dimension
1. The European Defence Equipment Market — 57
2. The Negative Effects of EEC Member States' present policy on procurement — 60
3. Possible forms of cooperation between industry, procurement authorities and firms — 67
4. Requirements of a future policy on procurement and manufacture — 72
5. Likely problems — 74
6. The EEC's role — 77
7. Conclusions — 80

Part III: The Resolution of the European Parliament of 14 June 1978 — 82

Part IV: Data
1. Examples of European and Atlantic Procurement Cooperation — 84
2. Which is the appropriate institution? — 88
3. Defence-related industries – defence output and defence share of total output — 94
4. A possible structure for a European armaments procurement agency — 95

Foreword

by the Rt. Hon. Geoffrey Rippon, M.P. Chairman of the European Conservative Group in the European Parliament

In submitting his report to the European Parliament in June 1978, Egon Klepsch initiated one of the most significant developments which has taken place within the European Community in recent years. The Klepsch Report is remarkable, both for its analysis of the problems that have prevented the creation of an effective European armaments industry and for the fresh approach that it adopts in seeking a solution to these problems. It has lifted the debate within the Community above trivialities to high politics. The European Community is about politics or it is about nothing. The Klepsch Report has thrust a major political issue on to the centre of the stage.

The most striking feature of Egon Klepsch's report is the clear way in which it demonstrates that there is a direct link between Community industrial policy and effective cooperation in European armaments procurement. Thus the Community cannot achieve a meaningful common industrial policy unless this includes military as well as civil products. Bodies such as NATO and the Independent European Programme Group (IEPG), which are striving to attain effective arms procurement policies, cannot succeed unless they use the unique potential of the European Community to organise and structure the industrial aspects of armaments production.

Speaking in the European Parliament's debate on the Klepsch Report in Strasbourg in June 1978 I stressed my own support, and the support of the Conservative Group as a whole, for the report's conclusions on the need to include armaments procurement in the Community's industrial policy. I stated that in the search for new projects and new markets, firms in all the countries of the Community were competing with firms in the United States which enjoy the economies of scale. In the event, we are not only making an inadequate contribution to our own defence, we are also wasting money and resources, falling behind in civil projects and creating unemployment and long-term decline in vital industrial fields.

It is not just a question of defence policy, nor is it really a party political issue. As the German Government's white paper on defence in 1971/72 said:

> 'The German economy cannot afford to forego the benefits deriving from such defence projects (that is, projects involving a high degree of technological innovation), ... especially since national development of weapons and equipment as well as collaboration in international armaments projects are dependent on a high technological standard of our industry.'

That applies equally to the United Kingdom and to all other members of the Community.

On the other side of the Iron Curtain, Mr Brezhnev has said recently that it is science and technology that will play a significant role in East/West competition. And I believe he is right. In that competition we must consider how we in Europe, within the Atlantic Alliance, can bring our aggregate technology to bear. Hitherto we have depended, both in civil and military terms – and the two are indeed intertwined – far too much on unilateral United States efforts. There has thus been in Europe far too much waste, overlap and duplication and we can no longer ignore the urgent need for greater interoperability and standardisation. Lip-service has been paid to this principle for many years, but now we need a real commitment by Europe as well as by the United States.

President Carter has expressed his determination to secure a two-way street in procurement policy. The two-way street concept has now become official policy of the Alliance and the final communiqué adopted by the Alliance Summit held in London in May 1977 stated that 'the Allies are determined ... to develop a more balanced relationship between European and North American members of the Alliance in the procurement of defence equipment'.

Egon Klepsch's report gives a lead to the Europeans in opening up new ways in which the Europeans can create a structured European armaments industry which would be the basis of the European end of the two-way street. Without an organised European armaments industry there can be no two-way street. And what institution other than the European Community can organise this?

As Egon Klepsch stresses, we in Europe have to collaborate to match United States' technology and markets. Technology, when exploited on a European basis, could well provide us with the military advantage of guns and the social advantages of butter. As it is, one of the worst features of our economic, industrial and employment situation in Europe today is the way in which our failure to collaborate has relentlessly eroded our industrial and technological capacity.

Reserves are indeed being wasted on a colossal scale as we all duplicate our efforts. The United States Senate Armed Services Committee has estimated this waste of resources, in the arms procurement field, at between 10-15 billion dollars a year. This inevitably results in a drastic reduction of the combat effectiveness of the West's military resources.

At present, we have a situation in which the West is infinitely wealthier than the Soviet Union and its allies. The aggregate GNP of the NATO countries is almost three times as great as that of the Warsaw Pact countries. So it is a tribute to the Soviet Union that, even allowing for the fact that they have spent a higher percentage of GNP on defence, they have so organised their industrial capacity that Soviet equipment now outnumbers that stationed in the Community by nearly 3 to 1.

Although the United States can organise American firms to meet the equipment needs of a homogeneous market, absence of action by Members of the European Community to create a similar defence market will force increasing technological dependence by European firms on the know-how of the United States. The employment of large numbers in the Community's technologically based firms will be at risk and so the future wealth-creating potential of the Community may be stymied if the governments of the Member States frustrate, by their refusal to act, the growth of the Community's technologies.

The Community must also be able to organise itself so as to achieve economy of scale in the manufacture of defence equipment. How can the economics of French production of AMX 30 battle tanks, of possibly 150 tanks annually, or British Chieftan tanks of say 200 annually, be compared with an estimated production by the Soviet Union of 1,000 main battle tanks a year? The same is true for artillery and aircraft.

Neither is it any longer true, as we have so complacently said for many years, that the Soviet numerical advantage is offset by the superior quality of Western equipment. According to the United States Administration, recent Soviet tanks, missile systems and personnel carriers are equal to or better than comparable NATO equipment employed today.

So it seems to me that a European Community Council of Defence and Industry Ministers must make a political commitment to authorise design and development of the next generation of all types of equipment on the basis that this equipment can be manufactured to the same blueprints in all

Member States having the necessary facilities.

This means cooperation in designing a European institutional framework in which procurement production can be shared and the results of development spread over European technology. This is the compensatory factor which is required in return for national sacrifices.

It is hoped that the efforts already undertaken by the IEPG will prove fruitful before long, but as yet few concrete results have come out of its work. The fresh ideas advanced by Egon Klepsch[1], and fully backed in a supporting report by Tom Normanton, are in no way intended to interfere in work on procurement being carried out either in NATO or in the IEPG. The essential character of the Klepsch proposal is industrial.

Egon Klepsch makes it clear that the strategic, tactical and military requirements to be met by conventional weapons produced in the framework of a structured programme developed by the Community's members, must continue in the future, as in the past, to be drawn up by the military authorities. The Nine's contribution, on the other hand, should consist essentially in structuring European armaments production in such a way that the requirements set by the military authorities, whether in NATO, the IEPG or elsewhere, can be met efficiently, economically and rationally by a single coordinated Community armaments industry. This armaments industry must be seen as part of the Community's future common industrial policy.

In the European Parliament's debate on 13 June 1978 on the Klepsch Report and Tom Normanton's Opinion[2], the spokesmen for the Christian Democratic and European Conservative Groups, Mr Notenboom and myself respectively, expressed full support for the Klepsch and Normanton documents and for the accompanying motion for a resolution

---

[1] Who wishes to acknowledge the valuable help given to him by Michael Palmer, of the European Parliament's Secretariat, in the preparation of his report.
[2] Submitted on behalf of the Parliament's Economic Committee.

submitted to Parliament by Egon Klepsch on behalf of the Political Committee. On behalf of the Liberal Group Mr Berkhouwer also expressed full support for the Klepsch Report and the resolution.

The main opposition to the Klepsch Report in the debate came from the Socialist Group, whose principal spokesman was Mr Dankert. The central point of the arguments advanced by the Socialists was that the development and production of weapons systems is not a job for the Commission. Mr Dankert said that the Commission should have a completely different role – to ensure that the national defence ministers procure their weapons systems from European industry provided that the industry meets a number of conditions. He argued that the report ought primarily to have dealt with that problem.

The spokesman of the Communist Group was Mr Soury, but he spoke in the debate only on behalf of the French Communists, the Italian Communists being in favour on the ground that Europe's technology must be left competitive. He opposed the report and resolution on the grounds that the question of armaments cooperation fell under the responsibility of national parliaments and that the European Parliament was not competent to discuss defence questions. Finally, Mr Krieg, a French Gaullist, speaking on behalf of the European Progressive Democrats, also argued against the report on the grounds that there could be no industrial policy on armaments without there being a defence policy, and that defence lay outside the competence of both the European Parliament and of the Community as a whole.

Replying to the debate, in which many other speakers took part, Vicomte Davignon made an important speech expressing the view of the Commission. In reply to the argument that any question involving defence or security was outside the Community's competence, Vicomte Davignon clearly expressed the Commission's policy:

'This is not our view, nor, moreover, was it that of the authors of the Treaty, because it provides for certain customs duties on the importation of military material into the Community. This is ample proof that the Community is not *ipso facto* excluded from dealing with military matters.'

Vicomte Davignon indicated that the Commission intended to act in the sense of the draft resolution under debate. In doing so it would lay special emphasis on the significance of government orders for the development of new fields of research and the maintenance of industry in the armaments sector and in the development of certain technologies which Community Member States needed and which could be satisfactorily developed only on a joint basis.

The object was, therefore, one of finding out what action, whether in connection with research or with orders, would, if taken jointly, help to strengthen the Community's industrial structure. If the Commission established that government orders were an important factor in the development of the arms industry and would enable production to take place in conditions of competition, the Commission must go on to establish in what sectors such research and joint action should be carried out.

He then concluded:

'This is therefore what we must try to do; when the political and military decisions have been taken, the Community can take the industrial decisions. The division of responsibility is clear; there is no transfer of powers from one sphere to another, at least at this stage. In assuming responsibility for taking part in these preparations, we do not think we are stepping outside our legitimate powers.'

In the ensuing vote there was a large majority in favour of the resolution accompanying the Klepsch Report. The exact figures cannot be given since the vote was taken by a show of hands, but those in the chamber reckoned that the majority in favour of the resolution was about two-thirds.

More recently the European Parliament's right to develop proposals of this kind, and the Commission's right to respond positively to such proposals, has been challenged within the French

FOREWORD

National Assembly. Great interest has been, and is continuing to be shown in the Klepsch Report within the Alliance and, also, particularly within the IEPG, which has already held an initial exchange of views concerning the Klepsch proposals at the level of the National Armaments Directors.

The Defence Committee of the Western European Union Assembly has adopted a report, submitted by Julian Critchley M.P., expressing full support for the Klepsch proposals; and in Belgium the Foreign Minister, Mr. Simonet, has stated that his Government consider it 'desirable' that the institutions of the Community should pay attention to the armaments industries.

The Klepsch Report has brought new life and fresh ideas into the old and sterile debate concerning European arms procurement cooperation. It is the beginning of a new road ahead, a road that must be travelled if we are to construct that European armaments industry without which the two-way street cannot be achieved.

Geoffrey Rippon

Luxembourg
OCTOBER 1978

THE KLEPSCH REPORT

Part I
Political Aspects

1. Common Industrial Policy

The real starting point of European defence procurement policy lies in the need to remedy the Community's continuing failure to develop a common industrial policy. Despite a number of initiatives, which now seem past history, such as the Joint Memorandum sent by the three Community executives to the Council of Ministers in March 1967 on Scientific and Technological Progress within the Community, and the Commission's memorandum on industrial policy ('The Colonna Plan'), little has, as yet, been achieved.

Although the Heads of Government themselves have referred to the need to move forward in the domain of industrial policy on a number of occasions, notably at the Copenhagen Summit of 14 and 15 December 1973, when they declared that the Community Member States should 'develop more actively between them a common policy on industrial, scientific and technological cooperation in all fields'[1] the only significant move made by the Community towards the establishment of part of a common industrial policy remains the Commission report and proposal to the Council for an action programme for the European aeronautical sector on whose main proposals the decisions of the Council are still awaited.

The report of Parliament's Economic and Monetary Affairs Committee on the Commission's document was adopted by Parliament on 6 July 1976.

Of particular interest in the context of the present report was the Commission's proposal in its document that the Member Governments, meeting

---
[1] Seventh General Report.

POLITICAL ASPECTS

in the Council, should consider the creation of a European military aircraft procurement agency. This proposal had already received a degree of support from the European Parliament, since the Parliament's resolution of 15 December 1975 urged the establishment of 'an agency ultimately aimed at the joint manufacture of weapons meeting the requirements of the Member States'. This proposal also coincides to some extent with that made by Mr Tindemans in his report on European Union, that consideration should be given to the setting up of a 'European Armaments Agency'. Mr Tindemans refers, also in his report, to 'the need to initiate a common industrial policy on the manufacture of armaments within the framework of the European Union'.

All the proposals made concerning the development of European armaments procurement cooperation in the present report are limited to conventional military equipment.

2. Attempts to achieve European Procurement Cooperation at the Atlantic Level

Why cooperation is necessary

There is nothing at all new or original in underlining the main reasons why it is necessary to achieve cooperation, within Europe, concerning the procurement of armaments. Quantities of ink have flowed on this intractable subject over many years. The need for cooperation has not only been felt at the European level but also in the wider framework of the North Atlantic Alliance, but this present report will concentrate on the need for action at the European level.

The symposium on a European Armaments Policy, organised by the Committee on Defence Questions and Armaments of the WEU Assembly, held in Paris on 3 and 4 March 1977, provided a good opportunity to take stock of the present situation and also the main perspectives of future action in the field of armaments procurement. The report of the WEU Assembly Defence Committee on 'A European Armaments Policy', which was based on the proceedings of the Symposium[1], points to three main reasons why cooperation in the armaments procurement field is necessary. First, financial. In a situation in which Western European national defence budgets are strictly limited, the increased sophistication and complexity of weapons systems has caused a dramatic escalation in costs. Long production runs and reduction of the cost to individual States of research and development are necessary. These can either be achieved through cooperation and joint armaments production programmes or, alternatively, through buying from a single source. Second, there is a military imperative. The military requirements are basically the complementary ones of interoperability and/or standardisation. Third, the report considers that there is a 'socio-economic' imperative – in practice a political imperative. This apparently combines the need to maintain the armaments industries of Western Europe, both so as to safeguard European independence and to maintain employment in this key sector.

One graphic instance of the lack of interoperability is that reported by 'Aviation Week' of 16 December 1974. During a NATO exercise in the North Atlantic held earlier in 1974, NATO forces themselves 'shot down' 30 of about 60 of their own aircraft, largely due to the communications systems of the Allied aircraft not being interoperable.

The Parliament's Political Committee wants to put forward new proposals and ideas which could, if implemented, provide a basis for effective action. If

---

[1] WEU Assembly Document 738 of 10 May 1977 (rapporteur: Mr Dankert).

this thought might be considered immodest, it wishes to emphasise that the proposals aim at changing the whole context of the armaments procurement problem by involving in it, for the first time, the European Community, which has the potential economic and commercial competences to organise the armaments industry, at the industrial level, to act effectively at the European level.

Before making proposals, it may be useful to describe and analyse briefly, the different attempts that are already being made, within different institutions, to achieve armaments procurement cooperation.

Independent European Programme Group

The most significant of the institutions, at the European level, is the Independent European Programme Group (IEPG). This came into being as a result of the initiative taken by the Eurogroup Defence Ministers in November 1975.[1] The result was the establishment of a new forum in which France could play a full part in cooperation in arms procurement and the development of a joint European position on which to discuss defence equipment questions with the United States. The significance of the word 'independent' is that the IEPG is independent of the Eurogroup.

The first meeting of IEPG at the level of Under-Secretaries of State, was held in Rome in February 1976. All the former Eurogroup countries have taken part in the IEPG since its inception, together with France.[2] At the Rome meeting, Italy was invited to chair the IEPG and it has held the chairmanship ever since. The second meeting of Under-Secretaries of State was held in Rome in

---

[1] The Eurogroup, an informal grouping of all the European members of the Alliance except France, was set up in November 1968 to strengthen the European contribution to the overall defence of the Alliance.
[2] Belgium, Denmark, Germany, Greece, Italy, Luxembourg, Netherlands, Norway, Turkey and the United Kingdom. Portugal joined in November 1976.

September 1976 and further meetings were held in 1977 and 1978. Between the meetings, held at the level of Under-Secretaries of State, occasional meetings are held at the level of national armaments directors. Meetings of experts have also been held. The expert meetings and the meetings of national armaments directors concern the progress of the different projects undertaken by the IEPG and prepare, also, the meetings of Under-Secretaries of State. The IEPG has no secretariat.

The main work and activities of the IEPG are divided between three panels:

Panel I,
under British chairmanship, is concerned with equipment planning. It is charged with confirming the future armaments requirements of the participating States, and the phasing out and phasing in of weapons systems. It has put together and agreed a schedule listing (a) equipment in service and (b) replacement intentions. This schedule will be brought up to date at regular intervals.

Panel II,
chaired by Belgium, coordinates the work of ten sub-groups which have been investigating the opportunities for cooperation in specific areas. It is considered, in IEPG circles, that four of the sub-groups hold out some hope of progress in the near future.[1] The other six exploratory groups are more experimental in nature and are trying to seek common ground for joint action.[2]

Panel III
is the Defence Economics and Procedures Panel, which is under German chairmanship. This panel has five sub-groups.

---

[1] These sub-groups concern MBT-105 improved ammunition, tactical combat aircraft, short-range unguided anti-tank weapons, and mine hunters.
[2] These exploratory groups' concerns are fast patrol boats, lightweight torpedoes, military helicopters, medium to long-range guided or unguided anti-tank weapons, portable surface-to-air guided weapons, and army mine systems.

Sub-Group 1: project procedures: attempts to obtain joint procedures for the development of new weapons systems, such as a common monitoring procedure.

Sub-group 2: compensation: considers the problems involved in intra-project balances and trade-offs.

Sub-Group 3: competition and transfer of technology and know-how: examines different national legislation concerning competition, technological transfers, sales.

Sub-Group 4: industrial cooperation, which is chaired by France, is a particularly important sub-group which tries to determine national armaments production capacities and, also, how to rationalise production.

Sub-group 5: arms exports: examines different national laws and regulations concerning armaments exports and problems raised by bans on armaments sales. It tries to determine how far there is a common approach concerning these questions.

The IEPG is as informal in character as the complexity of its work and objectives permits; for example, it has no central secretariat. It is working towards:

(a) harmonising national equipment schedules and replacement dates;
(b) agreeing on joint projects;
(c) eliminating duplication of development efforts.

To this end the Panels and subgroups described above have been established: and the necessary technical work is carried out by designated groups of experts in these bodies who report to the meetings of National Armaments Directors. This enables progress to be monitored at regular intervals. The National Armaments Directors in their turn report to Under Secretaries of State.

The IEPG has not yet reached the stage of having to take major decisions on specific projects. This has still to come; but as already indicated, work is proceeding in a number of fields. In particular, effective procedures have been established by

Panel I for identifying potential collaborative projects at an early stage. Machinery also exists in Panel II for examining these projects in greater detail with a view to deciding the nature and extent of collaborative work. In addition, Panel III has embarked upon a number of important studies in the complex area of national administrative and legal provisions and the organisation of defence industries with a view to furthering the establishment wherever possible of common procedures.

This is an extension of the work already carried out by EURONAD with the ultimate aim of:
 (a) permitting the effective use of funds for research development and production;
 (b) increasing standardisation and interoperability;
 (c) ensuring the maintenance of a healthy European defence industrial and technological base;
 (d) strengthening the European factor in the relationship with the United States.

It will not be possible to judge the effectiveness of the work of the IEPG or the degree of political commitment of its participating governments until the work of the subgroups leads to action.

The two words 'independent' and 'European' underline the separate identity of the IEPG. There are, nonetheless, aspects of the work of IEPG which are related to the work carried on within the Alliance on armaments procurement cooperation at the Atlantic level. Thus Admiral Mainini[1] told the WEU symposium held in Paris in March 1977, that the members of the IEPG 'have not neglected the wider consideration of relations with the countries on the other side of the Atlantic, particularly since the United States is increasingly and practically disposed to envisage standardisation as an aim to be achieved through a more balanced exchange between the two components of the Alliance'. The Conference of National Armaments Directors is

---

[1] Deputy Chief of the Italian Defence Staff, Chairman of the IEPG at National Armaments Director level.

regarded as the appropriate forum for exchanges of views and experience between IEPG members and other members of the Alliance.

It is only if the French and British armaments industries are included within one cooperative system that European armaments cooperation can succeed. With France taking part in its work as a full member, IEPG is seen, by the other participating countries, as having to succeed. If IEPG fails to achieve effective cooperation in a significant number of projects, this could well mean the end of the road for the European armaments industry.

EURONAD

EURONAD (the National Armaments Directors Sub-Group of the Eurogroup) still exists and carries out a limited amount of work, though it is basically marking time. For most practical purposes EURONAD has now been replaced by IEPG, where all the participating governments now place the main emphasis.

EURONAD still retains at least two residual functions. It meets the day before meetings of CNAD (the Conference of National Armaments Directors of NATO) to examine agenda items with a view to determining whether there is a 'Eurogroup interest' in them. It also provides a useful general framework for the subsequent discussion of equipment matters at the twice-yearly ministerial meetings of the Eurogroup. Despite what has been, in practice, a take-over by IEPG of EURONAD's main functions, there is no question, at present, of abolishing EURONAD, which has an important public relations role to play, vis-à-vis the US Administration and Congress, since the Eurogroup, of which EURONAD is the armaments wing, must not appear to American eyes to be diminishing its role of promoting a more effective European contribution to the overall defence effort of the Alliance. If, for one reason or another, IEPG fails to make meaningful progress, or if it were to break down, EURONAD might, further, revive its former working role – though it cannot be emphasised too strongly that such a role would inevitably be a very limited and restricted one compared with the potential role of IEPG.

Western European Union (WEU)

The Standing Armaments Committee (SAC) of WEU was set up in 1955. Its secretariat and headquarters are in Paris, where the Committee meets four times a year. It maintains close contacts with the NATO Military Agency for Standardisation (MAS) and the FINABEL[1] Committee of Principal Military Experts.

The performance of the Standing Armaments Committee in laying down the criteria according to which new weapons should be developed, has been disappointing. WEU has not tried to create any kind of armaments pool between its Member States. The presence of France as a full member of WEU and thus of the SAC, from the beginning, has often been considered an advantage. Those in WEU circles stress that the provisions set out in Article 5 of the Brussels Treaty[2] (which lays down the mutual defence commitments by which its members are linked) both go further than the comparable provisions of the North Atlantic Treaty – being completely automatic – and are more binding.

The main recent development in the work of the SAC has been the decision taken by the Council of WEU in May 1976 assigning to the Standing Armaments Committee a study of the armaments industries in Member Countries. This study will be made available to the IEPG. Apparently, this study

---

[1] The activities of FINABEL are described later. The word 'FINABEL' derives from the initial letters of its members – France, Italy, Netherlands, Federal Republic of Germany (Allemagne), Belgium and Luxembourg.
[2] The Treaty which established the former Brussels Treaty Organisation in 1948 and which, when revised in 1954, transformed the Brussels Treaty Organisation into Western European Union.

will not duplicate any work carried out by the IEPG.

FINABEL

FINABEL was set up following an initiative taken by the French Chief-of-Staff in 1953. It was at first composed of the Chiefs-of-Staff of the land forces of France, Italy, Belgium, Netherlands and Luxembourg. Germany joined in 1956 and the United Kingdom in 1972.

The aim of FINABEL is to encourage cooperation between its members concerning land armaments in the following respects: definition of qualitative requirements of military equipment and joint definition of the military characteristics of such equipment; joint testing of equipment and procedures; tactical and logistic studies; exchange of information.

FINABEL's work along these lines influences decisions taken by governments in the joint production of equipment. FINABEL's work is also of use, within the framework of the Alliance, to the NATO Army Armaments Group (NAAG) of CNAD. There are close contacts between FINABEL and the Standing Armaments Committee of WEU and also between FINABEL and Eurolong-term, the sub-group of the Eurogroup responsible for tactical concepts. The small secretariat of FINABEL has its headquarters in the Belgian Ministry of Defence in Brussels.

NATO

Although the present report concentrates on the problems of European Armaments procurement, these are related to work concerning weapons procurement carried out within the framework of the Alliance, and it therefore seems useful briefly to describe the main activities carried on within the Alliance in the procurement field.

There are three parts of the institutional machinery of the Alliance which play a major role in armaments policy. First, the staff specialists of the allied military commanders. Second, the civilian organisation and supporting secretariat. Here the principal body is the Conference of National Armaments Directors (CNAD). Third, under the Military Committee, there is an international staff and certain agencies, such as the Military Agency for Standardisation (MAS).

(a) C.N.A.D.

CNAD is the main civilian body working under the North Atlantic Council concerned with defence equipment. All members of the Alliance, including France, take part in its work. The three main working groups under CNAD are: the Naval Armaments Group; the Army Armaments Group, and the Air Force Armaments Group. Three further groups exist: the Defence Research Group, the Tri-Service Group on Air Defence and the Tri-Service Group on Communications and Electronics Equipment.

The three principal working groups which deal respectively with armaments for the Army, Navy and Air Force, hold exchanges of views between national staffs which attempt to find common areas of interest between two or more countries concerning the replacement of weapons systems that are to be phased out or the development or purchase of new weapons systems. Thus, three governments have cooperated on the MRCA (Multi-Role Combat Aircraft) and there has also been trilateral cooperation concerning 155 mm. F.H.–70 howitzers.

Within CNAD the procedure is that military requirements have to be agreed first between the countries interested in taking part in a specific equipment project. Then, in some cases, NIAG (the NATO Industrial Advisory Group) carries out a pre-feasibility study from the strictly technical point of view. Following this a wider feasibility study is carried out by the industries of the participating countries. This phase is governed by a Memorandum of Understanding (MOU). Resulting from the feasibility study, the NATO Operational Requirement is agreed by the countries concerned and a new MOU for the project definition, development and production phases is prepared. A NATO Steering Committee is then established by CNAD to complete the work and monitor the development of the project. All MOU's are between the Governments concerned. Industrial firms set up their own organisation.

CNAD is also competent in the field of procurement when two or more countries wish to purchase a certain item of equipment or weapons system from a third country. The present trend is to activate cooperative efforts for the development of new equipment from the earliest conceptual stage. But as far as the development of new equipment is concerned, the industries themselves have considerable autonomy. The main problems which have to be resolved in this lengthy and complex process are those resulting from the different logistic systems employed by different States and, also, problems of compensation and industrial trade-offs, and that of intellectual property rights.

(b) AGARD and MAS
The main body on the military side promoting the exchange of technological information amongst member countries of the Alliance is the Advisory Group for Aerospace Research and Development (AGARD). The Military Agency for Standardisation (MAS) also works under the Military Committee. The MAS issues Standardisation Agreements (STANAGS) concerning the procedures, doctrines and equipment characteristics to provide inter-operability or compatibility. The French Government is apparently prepared to accept STANAGS as the basis for equipment so long as such equipment is interoperable rather than standardised.

It is also important to note the activities of the Ad Hoc Committee on Equipment Interoperability which was set up within the Alliance in December 1975 in order to solve interoperability problems in some specific areas.

The Ad Hoc Committee works within the framework of the international secretariat of NATO, on the civilian side. In July 1976, a new body, the Armaments Standardisation and Interoperability Division, was set up as a part of the International Military Staff on a 2-year trial basis. The existence of this new body was reviewed in July 1978. The Chairman of the MAS is also the Chief Official (Assistant Director) of the Armaments Standardization and Interoperability Division.

3. Some Problems

The problems that make it difficult to develop effective European armaments procurement cooperation are many and complex. Their *detailed* analysis is the work of more specialised fora than Parliament's Political Committee, and in this respect tribute must be paid to the valuable work carried out over the years by the Committee on Defence Questions and Armaments of the WEU Assembly and the Military Committee of the North Atlantic Assembly, and its Sub-Committee on Defence Cooperation.

Nonetheless, it might be useful to indicate, here, some, at least, of the main problems which have to be solved if progress is to be made.

First, some of the economic problems, which are touched on only lightly. The fundamental problem that confronts Western European Governments in arms procurement is the recurrent one of having to choose between an American item of equipment which, with a long production run and a large home market, can be sold less expensively than a comparable European item, or a European system which – although helping to maintain the existence of the European armaments industry, and helping to maintain the competitiveness of European technology, and maintaining or creating jobs for European workers – will generally cost considerably more in view of the likelihood of there being a shorter production run and comparatively limited possibilities of export sales.

There are a number of ways of achieving standardisation. First, through the decision to buy one system or direct purchase. This saves the expense of research and development and a production base, and provides both economies of scale and standardisation. But it means that there can only be one winner in any given field of armaments, with all other countries and producers being losers. This is clearly unacceptable in political terms. Then there is production under licence, which alleviates some of the economic disadvantages but not all, particularly the lack of a research and development base, and can result in higher costs. Then there is competitive research and development with licensed coproduction. This alleviates the economic disadvantages already referred to but certainly leads to higher costs, as, for instance, with the F.16 aircraft.

Then there is cooperative research and development which is ideal, in principle, but concerning which it is very difficult to get joint agreement on requirements and schedules. But with lead times of 8 to 12 years, there can be no rapid results. This poses a special political problem, since this kind of time scale goes far beyond the foreseeable life of any one government or elected parliament. Unfortunately, little political credit can be gained by politicians planning projects of this kind which are, in any case all the more vulnerable to changes of political direction when their life span covers a period of time in which parliaments are re-elected and new governments take office.

Finally, there is the possibility of setting both short- and long-term goals and pursuing them concurrently, thus creating a broadly based group of winners able to absorb the occasional loss.[1]

---

[1] With Alliance expenditure currently of the order of $35 billion (U.S.) per year on conventional weapons development and production, it should not be impossible to create a group of winners. (1 billion U.S. = 1,000 million).

Then there is the related question of 'standardisation' and 'interoperability'. Although a number of governments consider that standardisation is more effective in terms of military operational efficiency, and in terms of improving logistic credibility, the French viewpoint is very different. Addressing the WEU symposium in Paris in March 1977, General Cauchie[1] explained that French armaments specialists preferred the approach of 'interoperability'. He argued, against standardisation, that through reducing the number of different types of military equipment used by the allied forces, this would simplify the task of an enemy in finding counter-measures, whereas if an enemy had to face interoperable but different equipment, he would have to have at his disposal a very much larger number of counter-measures.[2] Standardisation would also bring about an undesirable degree of specialisation of industries of countries in different types of military equipment. This would have an inevitable impact on employment, and would lead to monopolies or quasi-monopolies in the production of 'standardized' items.[3] Implicit in French opposition to standardisation is the fear that the standardized item of equipment will always be the American item.

Finally, General Cauchie drew attention to the vital consideration that a move to standardisation would involve an unacceptable relinquishment of

---

[1] Directeur adjoint à la Direction des Affaires Internationales, Délégation Générale pour l'Armement.

[2] Here it should be recalled that one of the main elements of the Warsaw Pact's superiority over NATO in terms of equipment is generally supposed, in the West, to be due to the standardised equipment used by the Warsaw Pact. If General Cauchie is right, the prevalent Western view must be wrong. However, it is interesting to note that, with their modernisation programmes, the Warsaw Pact countries are, apparently, beginning to destandardise their equipment.

[3] As far as the employment question is concerned, Thomas A. Callaghan Jr. the US independent armaments expert, in testimony before Congress, (Congressional Record, 1 July 1976) has stated that: 'If we can get this 'two-way street' working between Europe and the United States, both the United States and Europe will benefit economically in terms of business and jobs since the total market for military equipment of all the NATO allies is much greater than the individual market in one of the NATO allies'.

national sovereignty in the defence area. In favour of interoperability, General Cauchie stated that it was unnecessary to achieve standardisation when military equipment was interoperable: 'For example, provided a military aircraft can land on most bases, replenish its fuel tanks and ammunition and have no trouble in its telecommunications, it is effectively 100% operable. Who cares whether it has the same wing span or the same number of turbine blades as its competitors?'[1]

General Cauchie drew attention to the flexibility permitted by Standardisation Agreements (STANAGs) in allowing the development of several competitive systems. The standards agreed within this system permitted both interoperability and competition between different industries and different countries.

General de Mazière,[2] putting the point of view shared by Germany and a number of other countries, put the contrary case at the WEU symposium, arguing that interoperability was only of passing use as a means of moving on to the ultimate goal of standardisation. Specifically it was more expensive than standardisation. He thus pleaded in favour of standardisation, at least where the development of new weapons systems was concerned.

It does not seem useful to express a preference for one or other of these two methods of cooperation, apart from cautiously reflecting that whereas interoperability is the best we can do with the mess that presently exists, standardisation offers the most economic way of avoiding a mess in the future. If France insists on interoperability

---

[1] Official Record of the WEU European Armaments Policy Symposium. It could be objected here that the pilot would care a great deal if he had a defective turbine blade which could not be repaired because the base had non-standard blades in its depot. The plane would be interoperable as to fuel, ammunition and communications, but non-operable because of a standardisation failure.

[2] Former Inspector General of the Bundeswehr.

rather than standardisation for those projects in which she might take part in IEPG, this will clearly have a considerable influence on the way in which European procurement cooperation develops. Short-term, interoperability does not necessarily rule out the achievement of standardisation in the long-term. Fundamentally, it is more useful to regard interoperability and standardisation as complementary approaches rather than as rival or hostile ones.

A further problem is the difficulty of obtaining an efficient distribution of contracts and employment under the present system – or lack of system – of *ad hoc* cooperative projects run according to the principle of the 'juste retour'. Only when cooperation is systematic and organised on a long-term basis with compensation and trade-offs arranged on a wider and more flexible basis than at present, can it really prove its advantages.

But the most intractable problems are not economic but political and historic. Over the years the different countries of Europe have evolved separate strategic and tactical concepts as a result of their different national experiences in warfare over the centuries and as a result of different types of terrain and climatic conditions. An additional difficulty in the present situation is posed by the choice concerning the development of different types of new weapons which could be appropriate in defending Western Europe – particularly to enable infantry to repel tank or aircraft attacks – in the light of the experience of the most recent Middle East War. Will it be easy to obtain agreement between Governments on developing, jointly, appropriate new weapons of this type?

Thus, from the very start of attempts to achieve European armaments cooperation, one of the main difficulties has been how to persuade different countries to agree on the joint strategic and tactical concepts which would alone permit the development of standardised or interoperable military equipment. This difficulty still remains despite the attempts made to overcome it in

POLITICAL ASPECTS

EUROLONGTERM[1] and elsewhere.

Politically, the determining factor is national sovereignty and how far individual governments are prepared to go in compromising their national sovereignty in order to achieve a system which can be developed, bought and operated jointly by them and other interested governments.

A further political problem is that some European citizens might oppose the development of closer European armaments procurement cooperation, let alone the establishment of a European armaments industry, on the grounds that this was politically undesirable – particularly if the profitability of European armaments production were dependent on exports to third countries, notably developing countries.

The problem of which countries should or should not be permitted to import European armaments already exists, and is at present mainly a matter for decision by the governments of the arms manufacturing countries. It is possible that constraints and checks on arms sales to third countries will increase in the light of intensified European cooperation, rather than decrease. In this context it is worth noting the view expressed in paragraph 15 of Mr Dankert's report to the WEU Assembly of May 1977: 'The Committee believes that together, the European countries of the Alliance provide an arms market large enough for economic production that would be independent of exports to the Third World, thus enabling such exports to be terminated or limited to those deemed to be in the interest of Europe according to a commonly defined external policy'.

---

[1] EUROLONGTERM is the sub-group of the EUROGROUP concerned with tactical concepts and staff targets.

4. The U.S. Challenge

Traditionally the United States has dominated arms sales within the Atlantic Alliance, even though the American share of the military equipment of the European members of the Alliance has steadily declined since the 1960's. Addressing the WEU Symposium in Paris in March 1977, General Cauchie claimed that there is, at present, an adverse balance of approximately 10-1 between US exports to and imports from Western Europe in defence equipment, the ratio being as high as 40-1 in the case of France.

Historically the US Government has, for strategic and political reasons, proceeded in what Mr Dankert's report to the WEU Assembly describes as 'a policy of near autarchy in weapons procurement'. In particular, the Buy American Act has protected the American market to the level of 50% of domestic costs in the case of defence equipment. When the US does purchase European equipment, such as the Roland Guided Weapon or the Harrier vertical take-off aircraft, agreements for manufacture under licence in the US are demanded.

But there have been some recent official moves by the US Administration and Congress. Attention was drawn to a number of these in the recent report of the Georgetown University Center for Strategic and International Studies on the proceedings of a seminar organised by the Center, entitled 'Allied Partnership in Armaments' of March 1977.

First, Section 814(a) of the Department of Defence Appropriation Authorisation Act of 1976, was amended, following initiatives taken by Senators Culver and Nunn, in the following sense: 'It is the policy of the United States that equipment procured for the use of personnel of the Armed Forces of the United States stationed in Europe under the terms of the North Atlantic Treaty should be standardized or at least interoperable with equipment of other members of the North Atlantic

Treaty Organisation'. The Secretary of Defence was authorised, by the Culver/Nunn amendment, to determine that procurement of such equipment from the United States source 'is inconsistent with the public interest'. The Secretary of Defence is obliged, under the Culver/Nunn amendment, to report to Congress concerning any case in which he initiates procurement action "of a new major system which is not standard or interoperable with equipment of other members of the North Atlantic Treaty Organisation".

Section 803 of the same Act was amended, following action taken by Senators Culver and Nunn, to include the following most significant declaration: 'It is the sense of the Congress that progress toward the realisation of the objectives of standardisation and interoperability would be enhanced by expanded inter-Allied procurement of arms and equipment within the North Atlantic Treaty Organisation. It is further the sense of the Congress that expanded inter-Allied procurement would be facilitated by greater reliance on licensing and coproduction agreements among the signatories of the North Atlantic Treaty.' But Congress stressed, in amending the same Section, that licensing and coproduction agreements must be properly constructed, 'so as to preserve the efficiencies associated with the economies of scale'.

Finally, paragraph (c) of Section 803 of the same Act was amended to include another important declaration: 'It is the sense of the Congress that <u>standardisation of weapons and equipment within the North Atlantic Alliance on the basis of a 'two-way street' concept of cooperation in defense procurement between Europe and North America could only work in a realistic sense if the European nations operated on a united and collective basis. Accordingly, the Congress encourages the governments of Europe to accelerate their present efforts to achieve European armaments collaboration among all European members of the Alliance.</u>'

Also of great significance was the report published by the Center for Strategic and International Studies of Georgetown University in September 1975 by Thomas A. Callaghan Jr. entitled 'US/European Economic Cooperation in Military and Civil Technology'. The study was originally prepared in August 1974 under State Department contract, with funds provided by the Defence Research Projects Agency and the Department of the Air Force.

In his report, Mr. Callaghan analysed the way in which the member countries of the North Atlantic Alliance spent some $120 billion (US) a year on the development, production, training, maintenance and operational support of general purpose forces which should provide a credible military capability, sufficient to maintain a conventional military balance with the Warsaw Pact. <u>In Mr. Callaghan's view the lack of coordination, together with duplication and waste of resources has resulted in a situation in which this enormous expenditure does not provide the Alliance with an adequate military capability.</u>

Waste and duplication in research and development and loss of economy of scale in equipment production, together with inefficient and differing systems of logistics, were pin-pointed by Mr Callaghan as the main reasons for the poor performance of members of the Alliance concerning military procurement. Outstanding amongst the many recommendations contained in Mr Callaghan's report was the proposal that a single transatlantic market in defence equipment should be set up involving not only a 'two-way street' in military equipment but, also, the establishment of a European Defence Procurement Agency.

Following the publication of the Callaghan Report, there was rapid action at governmental level. Thus, following NATO's Defence Planning Committee meeting of December 1974, the British Defence Minister, Mr Roy Mason, was able to describe the situation, in addressing the House of

Commons, as follows: 'There was general agreement – and in this I include my colleague the US Defence Secretary – that progress on standardisation of equipment must involve genuine two-way traffic between the European allies and the United States. At the DPC meeting last week I thought it was a break-through that the United States Defence Secretary should at least acknowledge that principle.'

The Eurogroup countries then, at their meeting of 7 May 1975, made standardisation of armaments their main topic and indicated, in the communiqué published by the Eurogroup Defence Ministers that they awaited a US Government response to the so-called 'Eurogroup proposals'. The American response was not long delayed. At the meeting of the Defence Planning Committee in Brussels of 22/23 May 1975 the participating ministers agreed, including US Defence Secretary Schlesinger, 'to pursue within the appropriate machinery the establishment of a 'two-way street' between Europe and North America, in order to provide a more cost-effective use of resources and increase standardisation of weapon systems'.

But although the US thus accepted, formally, the concept of the 'two-way street', Mr Schlesinger made it clear, at that time, to the European members of the Alliance, that the US Government was not interested in buying from Europe military equipment which did not meet her own military requirements or which she could make more cheaply herself.

In his study for the International Institute for Strategic Studies, Mr D.C.R. Heyhoe comments: 'The onus was therefore on the Europeans to put their own house in order, and to make such arrangements as would enable them to compete realistically with American industry'.[1] Mr Heyhoe described the rôle of the Callaghan Report in these developments as being: '... probably that of a catalyst which not only reflected avowed Con-

---

[1] 'The European Programme Group', Adelphi Paper, No.129

gressional concern at the waste of resources through lack of standardisation, but also held obvious appeal for the European Allies with its proposals for increased American purchases of European equipment'.

At the Summit meeting of the North Atlantic Alliance held in London on 10 May 1977, President Carter stressed the need for members of the Alliance to 'use limited resources wisely'. He stressed the need to 'improve cooperation in development, production and procurement of Alliance defence equipment. The Alliance should not be weakened militarily by waste and overlapping. Nor should it be weakened politically by disputes over where to buy defence equipment. ... We must make a major effort to eliminate waste and duplication between national programmes: but provide each of our countries an opportunity to develop, produce and sell competitive defence equipment, and to maintain technological excellence in all allied combat forces.'

Specifically, President Carter laid down three aims. First, 'The United States must be willing to promote a genuine two-way trans-Atlantic trade in defence equipment ... Second, I hope the European allies will continue to increase cooperation among themselves in defence production ... Third, I hope that European and the North American members of the Alliance will join in exploring ways to improve the development and procurement of defence equipment. This joint examination could involve the European Programme Group as it gathers strength and cohesion.'

Enlarging on the theme of the 'two-way street' President Carter stated that the 'Administration's decisions about the development, production and procurement of defence equipment will be taken with careful attention to all the interests of all members of the Alliance. I have instructed the Secretary of Defence to seek increased opportunities to buy European defence equipment where this would mean more efficient use of Allied resources. I will work with the Congress of the

United States to this end.'

Also in his speech, President Carter called for proposals by the Defence Ministers of the members of the Alliance to submit a long-term defence programme to strengthen the Alliance deterrence and defence in the 1980's, to a summit meeting to be held in Washington in the spring of 1978. He hoped that the Defence Ministers would already be able to make an interim report to the Ministerial meeting of the North Atlantic Council in December 1977.

In view of the great emphasis placed by President Carter on the more rational and effective procurement of military equipment in his speech, it is clear that the Defence Ministers are expected, in submitting their programme to the Alliance summit meeting in the Spring of 1978, to bear procurement in mind, even if the European allies are not ready, by that date, to advance definitive proposals concerning procurement cooperation.

On the question of how to obtain a more efficient use of Alliance resources, Mr Thomas A. Callaghan Jr. has argued, in testimony given to the US Congress on 21 July 1977, that the United States itself can no longer fund its own arms developments programmes adequately, with the result that many arms projects crawl along or become obsolete before they can be completed. In his view the United States needs Europe to undertake many such projects so that these, wherever undertaken, could be fully funded and move to completion. In other words, what is required for the proper arming and equipping of Alliance forces, including those of the United States, is the spreading of the technology base to Europe.

It is for Member Countries of the IEPG and other appropriate institutions, including the European Community, to develop an appropriate response to President Carter's challenge. One of the aims of the present report is to contribute to the proposals that the Europeans could make in responding to this challenge.

The final communiqué adopted by the London summit stated in paragraph 4 that, 'the Allies are determined to cooperate closer in all aspects of defence production. Their aims are to achieve the most effective use of available resources and to preserve and promote the strong industrial and technological capability which is essential for the defence of the Alliance and to develop a more balanced relationship between European and North American members of the Alliance in the procurement of defence equipment. The means of deepening this cooperation should be reviewed in appropriate fora.'

5. Collaborative Projects

Although the present report generally stresses the need to achieve more consistently organised and structured European cooperation in arms procurement, this does not mean that there have not been a number of successful examples of procurement cooperation in the past, or that progress is not being made in a number of specific areas at present.

It is impossible to judge the overall effectiveness of the collaborative projects so far undertaken in Europe without being simplistic, but it may be useful to quote some judgements made concerning European armaments procurement by Mr Roger Facer in his IISS Study[1] and the WEU Defence Committee Report of May 1977 concerning 'European Armaments Policy'.

Mr Facer states: 'There can be little doubt that collaboration has generally been a practical success, at least in relation to the objectives set. The projects have not been immune from delays and costs increases, some of which may be attributed to the fact that the projects are joint ones, but it would be absurd to blame all the misfortunes of a collaborative project on collaboration itself. It is

---

[1] 'Weapons Procurement in Europe – Capabilities and Choices'.

also misleading to regard collaboration as an expensive way of procuring equipment. No doubt in an ideal world cheaper methods could be found; but when the alternative is, as it usually is, a purely national project, the development-cost savings to an individual country from collaboration outweigh the higher total costs of the project, which are jointly borne. Estimates of the extra cost of collaboration in a project vary: the development cost may be 20% more if the project is divided conventionally, or up to 50% more if several versions of the equipment are produced to meet differing national requirements. The cost of production will probably also be higher, because the equipment will have some features upon which one partner insists and which the other does not strictly need. But simple arithmetic will show that collaborative development will still be the cheaper solution for a country unless its total production requirements are very large: for example, an advanced combat aircraft costing a country $1,000 million in total to develop and $5 million each to produce would be more cheaply produced in partnership (assuming a 'collaboration premium' of 20% in both development and production costs) unless more than 400 aircraft are required. There are other financial advantages. The investment in the project is nearly halved in the earlier development and production-tooling stages, the higher costs occurring later; this makes for greater flexibility, especially if the total numbers to be bought are uncertain at the outset. Collaboration brings the advantage that research and development resources, both human and financial, can be spread over a greater number of projects. Risks of failure are shared. Technology is diffused without a corresponding increase in scientific and industrial resources. In short, the cost of developing advanced modern weapon systems is now so high in relation to the numbers required by European countries that collaboration is essential, unless one is prepared to gamble on securing large enough export markets.'

It is interesting to note that Mr Facer points to two serious practical problems which might inhibit future collaboration. First, the lack of effective machinery for agreeing common staff requirements. Second, the difficulty of harmonising the time-scale of equipment replacement, partly because the smaller countries often make do with equipment long since considered obsolete by the larger nations, and partly because national priorities differ. Once a country gets out of step with others, it may take decades to get back in.

From his point of view, the rapporteur of the WEU Defence Committee, Mr Dankert, quotes one of the rapporteurs of the WEU Symposium[1] as listing the advantages of industrial cooperation in European weapons production as being: (a) sharing of development costs; (b) sharing of development risk; (c) broadening of background: experience, capacity; (d) reduction of procurement cost, larger quantity and cadence; (e) advantage in logistics and readiness to act. And he cites the disadvantages as: (i) coordination of different national regulations, standards and procedures; (ii) only partial activation of industrial potential.

On the industrial management front, Mr Dankert's report for the WEU Defence Committee pointed out that, 'The Panavia joint *industrial* consortium ... and attendant management agencies NAMMA/NAMMO represents the kind of industrial and official administrative collaborative evolution which could set the pattern for future joint weapon development and production in Europe ... It is just the type of successful military collaborative consortium which Mr Greenwood[2] warned the symposium should not be broken up when its own particular programme is completed. He advised the addition of further partners to such consortia and the assignment to them of additional programmes as they occur.'

Concerning the costs of collaboration, the WEU

---

[1] Mr Kuhlo, Head of Dynamics Division, Messerschmitt-Bölkow-Blohm.
[2] Then Chairman of British Aircraft Corporation.

Assembly Report found, on its side, that 'It is difficult to quantify the cost effects of collaboration. However, it seems that by doubling the market due to collaboration, a saving on the mean unit cost in the order of 20% is achieved on a major military aircraft programme. On smaller projects, the saving might be about 10% per unit. These figures are based on estimates for national bilateral programmes in which, although the total development bill in collaboration is one and a half times that of the unilateral bill, each sponsoring government has to find only two-thirds of the money required to do the job on its own. At the same time, a 5% increase in manufacturing costs arises from the difficulties of geographical distance, language difference and so on.'

6. The Community and European Armaments Procurement

Efforts made by European countries to cooperate concerning arms procurement, both bilateral and multi-lateral, have represented a considerable advance over the situation in which the procurement of new military equipment was carried out by individual countries acting on their own. There is now a considerable amount of European cooperation concerning arms procurement, but this has been and continues to be on an *ad hoc* project-by-project basis. The attempts that have been made by the Eurogroup, WEU, FINABEL, and other bodies to achieve a consistent and more closely knit system of arms procurement have not succeeded. This has been so at the wider Atlantic level also.

Until recently one of the main reasons that prevented interested countries from achieving a greater degree of cooperation was the difference of political and institutional approach of France and of its partners. But the creation of the IEPG has provided a forum in which France and other European countries can work together concerning armaments procurement.

One of the other main reasons that has prevented the development of closer cooperation has been the fact that the military/political institutions engaged in arms procurement have lacked the potential capability of the Community to organise the industrial side of arms procurement and to create a structured single Western European armaments market.

This is where the European Community can play a significant rôle and make a vital contribution of a kind which is not possible for the other interested institutions, such as NATO, WEU, etc. The Commission's 'Action programme for the European aeronautical sector' was a first hint of what could be achieved by the Community if the Member Governments were agreed to promote positive steps in this sense.

Although the IEPG has already moved ahead fast in its work of defining areas where joint projects could be mutually profitable to interested governments, the IEPG is an informal grouping with no powers or competences to organise the economic and industrial aspects of arms cooperation. The Community, like the IEPG, has the great advantage of full French membership. It could also, in the development of the common industrial policy, which is a major goal for the future development of the Community, develop, at the level of the Nine, a structured, homogenous market for arms sales. Indeed, without the development of a single organised market for the armaments sector, it is hardly possible to imagine how a common industrial policy could be brought into being, particularly in view of the vital rôle that military production and sales play in the aircraft industry, shipbuilding and electronics. The Commission's action programme for the European aeronautical sector pointed out, in October 1975, for instance, that the military market accounted for 62% of aircraft industry sales by Community member states. A table included in

POLITICAL ASPECTS

Roger Facer's IISS study 'Weapons Procurement in Europe – Capabilities and Choices', London 1975, sets out the significant defence share of the total output for major defence-related industries in Britain, France and Germany for the years 1968 and 1969. In the electronics sector, advanced defence requirements, together with space, have been one of the main sources of new technological development in the past twenty years. In the United States, for a time in the mid-60s, the Government market for electronic products was larger than the entire commercial market in Europe. Defence systems probably account for no more than 7% of the market for electronic components, by value today, but it is far more important in terms of its impact on technological development. Moreover, a technical attempt to agree on a new systems philosophy for Europe in such cases could have a significant military impact. As a consequence, research programmes in industries such as aircraft and electronics are often concerned with developing advanced technologies which have both military and civil application. Supercritical wing technology, or very large scale integrated circuits will be relevant to both, and European programmes in such areas cannot accept an artificial borderline. Indeed, in both the aircraft and electronic industries, the survival of an independent European advanced military capability is made easier by the survival of the civil industry and for aircraft the reverse is even more true. Commercial policy towards the outside world, whether it be concerned with the Community's import tariff or with negotiations with the United States for modifications of the Buy American Act is also one integral issue, particularly for advanced technology industries. Employment in key industries is also the combined result of the requirements of military and civil markets. Thus the work load in the aircraft industry is a sensitive balance between military and civil programmes. The same is true for some shipyards.

In short, as far as the aircraft, shipbuilding and

electronics industries are concerned, it is not possible for the industries to survive without military as well as civilian work. The future of these industries can only be viewed as the development of overall civilian/military operations within each sector. If, then, these key industries are to remain technologically up-to-date and competitive, at the world level, any plans for the development of the common industrial policy must inevitably include the military as well as civilian sides of their work.

7. Conclusions and Proposals

The main general conclusion to be drawn is, in the light of the previous chapter, to call upon the European Commission to make proposals for the creation of a single, structured Community market in military equipment which would, taking into account the civilian aspects of the industries concerned, constitute a major element, or 'building block', in the development of an overall common industrial policy.

But the Community can only move in this direction within the context of parallel development in the IEPG and as part of the overall 'two-way street' relationship between Europe and the United States. It cannot work in isolation, ignoring the progress that is being made within IEPG and in the US/European dialogue concerning the 'two-way street' concept.

A number of proposals have been made, in recent years, concerning the creation of a European Armaments Procurement Agency. Mr Tindemans proposed that consideration should be given to the establishment of such an agency in his report on European Union. Mr Spinelli, when he was a Member of the Commission, called for the creation of a similar agency. Lord Gladwyn, in his report on the effects of a European Foreign Policy on Defence Questions, for Parliament's Political

Committee, put forward a similar proposal, and on the American side, Mr Thomas A. Callaghan, Jr. has also called for the creation of such an agency. Indeed, before the IEPG effectively took over the rôle of EURONAD, the Eurogroup Ministers went as far as commissioning, at The Hague, on 5 November 1975, a study of the tasks 'which a European Defence Organisation' might undertake.

Now that France is working together with its European partners within the framework of the IEPG, it would seem logical for the IEPG itself to become the main political and decision-making element – at ministerial level – of a European arms procurement agency.

The next conclusion to be drawn is, therefore, that the IEPG should be given a permanent secretariat which would work on the instructions of the Member Governments. The IEPG in its new form would provide the main institutional part of a European Armaments Procurement Agency.

In return for undertaking to develop the industrial and commercial aspects of European armaments cooperation, the Community would have to be represented alongside the individual participating governments, in the IEPG meetings.[1] According to one possible model, the Commission could represent the Community, with the responsible Commissioner participating alongside national defence ministers in ministerial meetings of the IEPG. But if this were not acceptable to all Member States of the Community, the appropriate minister of the country which held the Presidency of the Council could speak for the Community as an entity, with the Commission being represented at observer level. In the event of one or other present or potential Member States of the Community not wishing to accept this responsibility, the Community could, perhaps, be represented by a minister from the country which had just held or which was just about to hold the Presidency. In the

---

[1] Any technical difficulties presented by Article 223 of the EEC Treaty could perhaps be overcome by a 'gentlemen's agreement'.

event of the Commission filling the major rôle, it would have to remain in constant touch with the Council of the European Communities regarding its participation in the IEPG, and could work to a long-term mandate given to it by the Council. It should be answerable to the European Parliament concerning its rôle in arms procurement. The Presidency of the Council should agree to reply to questions tabled by members of the European Parliament in debates concerning the rôle of the Community in its relationship with the IEPG.

The next conclusion is, therefore, that the Commission and/or Presidency of the Council should represent the Community, as an entity, within the IEPG. Further, some members of the secretariat of the IEPG might be detached Community officials, working alongside officials from the Member countries of the IEPG.

The creation of a structure of this kind would provide a flexible institutional basis for a European Armaments Procurement Agency within which the Community could operate as an entity. The major political problems to be overcome would be, first, the precise rôle to be played by Ireland, as a neutral country and, second, the position of IEPG member countries which were not, or not yet, members of the Community, such as Greece, Norway, Portugal and Turkey.

The valuable experience of agencies which have already had a successful record in joint procurement, such as Panavia and NAMMA/NAMMO, should not be wasted. It might therefore be useful to build up, on the day-to-day management front, institutions derived from the most successful agencies of this kind. These agencies could be responsible to the IEPG and could receive political directives from its Ministers. On the industrial side, there would have to be links between these agencies, or bodies, on the one side, and industry on the other, within the context of a Community industrial policy. Some observers have suggested that the future structure of European arms procurement should be based mainly on the development of agencies of this type. But such an approach could lead to the continuation of uncoordinated ad hoc arrangements and experience has demonstrated the need for an overall view and administration of the European armaments industry. The adoption of the proposals made here would mean that instead of there being a proliferation of new agencies and bodies over the years, the same people would continue to build up an experience of handling and managing one cooperation project after another.

The next conclusion is, therefore, the need to select, in each major equipment cooperation sector, an appropriate management agency which, under the supervision of the IEPG and the Commission, would be responsible for the day-to-day management of individual projects.

The 'European Armaments Procurement Agency' constituted by the IEPG, the Community, the management agencies, etc., would presumably have, as one of its main tasks, the rôle of representing and negotiating for Europe in the 'two-way street' dialogue with the United States. But it could well be some time before the European armaments industry was sufficiently well organised and structured to be able to deal on equal terms with that of the United States. This does not mean, however, that a start cannot already be made to a meaningful dialogue between Europe and the United States and Canada concerning military procurement. There are a number of problems concerning trade in military equipment which already need discussion between Europe and the United States and Canada as a matter of urgency. These include the 'Buy American' Act, as modified by Congressional action, the Foreign Military Sales Regulations, bilateral M.O.U.s etc.

In this context, the development of the Community's common commercial policy provides a further reason why the Community, in general, and the Commission in particular, should be directly involved in the management and development of trade in armaments at the transatlantic level.

The conclusion to be drawn here is that the Commission should represent Community Member States (in agreement or consultation with other European States taking part in the IEPG) in negotiating with the US and Canadian Governments the commercial conditions governing trade in armaments at the transatlantic level.

When the IEPG and the Commission have succeeded in creating a structured market for the European armaments industry, the European Armaments Procurement Agency will be in a position to negotiate arms purchases and sales with the United States within the 'two-way street'. In order to reach this stage, it is considered essential for the IEPG, at ministerial level, to be able to take binding decisions concerning the types of weapons to be developed or purchased under the auspices of the Agency.

As Lord Gladwyn has already pointed out in his earlier report for the Political Committee, it is not possible to dissociate security from a European foreign policy. Thus, as both he and Mr Blumenfeld, in his report for the Political Committee on European Political Cooperation, have suggested, it might be useful to envisage the broadening, where appropriate, of European political cooperation meetings to include defence as well as foreign affairs ministers, and officials from national defence ministries as well as from national foreign ministries.

It is hoped that the institutional arrangements outlined above would meet the French requirement, as expressed by French spokesmen at, for instance, the WEU Symposium of March 1977, that the institutional basis of a more effective European defence effort should respect 'relevant national interests', as Mr Cristofini[1] General Rapporteur of the Symposium, stated, and whose proceedings should, as General Cauchie remarked at the Symposium, be 'conducted on pragmatic and flexible lines with no hard and fast structure and no

---

[1] Former President of the Société Nationale Industrielle Aérospatiale (SNIAS).

cumbersome and sterilizing mechanisms'.

At this point it is relevant to quote the four guidelines laid down by Mr Cristofini, the General Rapporteur of the WEU Symposium, for success in European industrial armaments policy: 'First, the institutional framework had to be sound to ensure that relevant national interests were preserved ... while working out joint industrial programmes. Secondly, profitability had to be ensured in cooperative projects. Mr Greenwood suggested in this regard that a 'common identity of purpose' was necessary. Thirdly, a degree of protection had to be introduced, at least in the early stages. And fourthly, resources had to be adequate to bring Europe nearer to the level of major powers in this field.'

The European Community is well equipped to play the major role in organising the industrial aspects of European equipment procurement. In particular, the Community has a considerable experience of organising solutions, within the widest economic and commercial context, to the problems of trade-offs and compensation, which are particularly acute in the realm of defence contracting.

The Community's experience in this respect, could usefully be brought to bear on these problems in the field of defence procurement. With the help of the type of institutional arrangement proposed above, it should, also, be possible to lift European procurement cooperation out of the present extremely limited project-by-project approach, based all too often on the restrictive economic principle of the *juste retour*, to a completely different dimension in which a whole variety of different projects could be viewed, by the participating governments and industries as part of a single overall complex of trade-offs and compensation. Further, as the Commission has already proposed for the aeronautic sector, Community financing should be available to develop the European armaments industry, or specific sectors of it, such as aircraft and ship construction or electronics. Only in ways of this kind can the European armaments industry hold its own with its American counterpart and can Europe, in the future, have a chance of avoiding the necessity of 'buying American', as in the case of the F-16, every time that major new systems have to be purchased. Further, only by developments of this kind will Western Europe be able to maintain an effective conventional capability vis-à-vis the Warsaw Pact, and to ensure that the level of the nuclear threshold does not fall even more dangerously low than it is now.

It is therefore proposed that the European Parliament should call upon the Commission to draw up an action programme, making specific proposals, concerning European equipment procurement, to be submitted to the Council. This programme would constitute a major step towards the creation of a common industrial policy.

The Commission should, after appropriate consultation, suggest how Ireland might best fit into or be associated with this programme. It might also investigate the potential relationship of Greece, Portugal and Spain to the suggested programme. <u>The Commission should, in its action programme, make proposals as to the financing by the Community of collaborative European procurement projects.</u> The Commission should also make proposals, in its programme, concerning both the institutional and commercial relations (for the products concerned) between Community States and European non-Community States taking part in the work of the Procurement Agency. Any modification of Article 223 of the EEC Treaty that might be considered necessary could be achieved by means of a 'gentlemen's agreement' between Member Countries.

Finally, it is to be hoped that European governments, on their side, will note and act on the suggestion made by Mr Thomas A. Callaghan Jr. in his report on 'US/European Economic Cooperation in Military and Civil Technology' that procurement cooperation should be treated as a high political priority and that a comparatively senior minister in each government should be given direct responsibility for procurement cooperation.

Part II
The Industrial Dimension

*(Comments on the Klepsch Report drafted by
Mr Tom Normanton M.P. on behalf of the
European Parliament's Committee on
Economic and Monetary Affairs)*

1. The European Defence Equipment Market

In 1976, world spending on defence amounted to US $276,000 million at 1973 prices. The USA spent US$77,000 million, while the total figure for the Member States of the Community was US $40,200 million, analysed in the table below.

Defence expenditure by Member States in 1976 (in US $ 000 million at 1973 prices and exchange rates)[1]

EUR-9	40.2
Belgium	1.5
Fed. Rep. of Germany	12.3
Denmark	0.7
France	10.4
Italy	3.7
Ireland	0.3[2]
Luxembourg	0.0[3]
Netherlands	2.1
United Kingdom	9.1

The table on the next page shows the spending by a number of members of the Atlantic Alliance on major purchases of equipment as a percentage of their overall defence expenditure, and from this we see that the Community countries for which figures

---

[1] Source: World armaments and disarmaments. SIPRI yearbook 1977.
[2] 1975.
[3] Defence expenditure for 1976: US $ 17 million.

are given spent between 10 and 20% of their 1977 defence budgets for this purpose, apart from Luxembourg with its very low figure. The figures must, however, be viewed with some reservation as they only cover 'major purchases of equipment', and it is often difficult to draw the line accurately between the purchase of equipment and expenditure on building and installations. In most cases, total spending on equipment would therefore be considerably higher than indicated in the table.

Spending on major purchases of equipment as a percentage of total defence expenditure

	1972	1973	1974	1975	1976	1977
	%	%	%	%	%	%
Belgium	11.4	8.4	8.8	9.1	11.1	10.3
Canada	6.1	7.3	5.9	6.3	8.0	9.1
Denmark	15.4	17.2	19.3	19.0	19.4	17.3
Fed. Rep. of Germany	12.3	12.1	11.9	11.8	13.2	13.3
Italy	16.9	15.2	15.2	13.9	13.1	14.0
Luxembourg	1.5	1.3	2.4	1.0	3.4	2.9
Netherlands	10.7	11.2	13.2	15.6	15.2	18.2
Norway	11.8	11.7	13.4	14.4	13.3	16.6
Portugal	7.5	4.5	3.1	1.9	1.9	2.2
Turkey	4.9	5.0	3.0			
U.K.	18.6	19.3	17.2	19.3	20.6	21.8
U.S.A.	21.6	18.9	18.1	17.5	18.5	20.8

Source: NATO

THE INDUSTRIAL DIMENSION

The armaments industries of the Federal Republic of Germany, France, Italy and the United Kingdom largely cover those countries' domestic requirements for all types of conventional defence equipment; combat aircraft, helicopters, tanks, various vehicles, artillery, small arms, missiles, warships, ammunition, etc. These countries obtain most of their armed forces' equipment from their own industries. For example, German industry produces 70% of the equipment used by the Bundeswehr. If we disregard warships, for which all countries apart from Luxembourg have their own production capacity, the other Member States have to import most of their requirements for defence equipment from the above-mentioned countries and the USA, and in some cases from other countries.

This division between four largely self-sufficient Member States and five which depend on imports, and a lack until recently of any coordination of imports have produced a situation in which the armed forces' equipment is not only not standardised, but for the most part not interoperable either. Military considerations alone make this an unsatisfactory situation.

However, in recent years the economic disadvantages of this fragmentation of the market have become more and more obvious: <u>the cost of defence equipment has increased far more than general rates of inflation. Tanks and combat aircraft frequently cost more than ten times as much in real terms as they did at the end of the Second World War.</u> As a result, simple economics have imposed cooperation in a number of cases, mainly in the production of military aircraft, which today, at prices of over US $ 10 million apiece (MRCA Tornado), are a particularly heavy burden on defence budgets. The extremely high R&D costs of advanced equipment in this price class makes it increasingly difficult to produce on economically acceptable terms for a single large European country's defence forces; this has made joint production between several countries an obvious solution.

An alternative solution has been national production combined with substantial exports. The disadvantage of this is that the maintenance of national production capacity comes to depend largely on other countries' procurement policies; and there is likely to be less and less room for political manoeuvre on arms exports.

A survey undertaken by the US Department of Defense shows that in 1974 France was the biggest arms exporter in the Community, with total exports of US $ 3,000 million, followed by the UK with 1,500 million, Italy with 240 million and the Federal Republic of Germany with 180 million, while none of the other Member States exported arms in any quantity. We must assume that, to France and the United Kingdom, exports are essential if they wish to maintain the present structure of their defence industries.

All in all it is clear that present cooperation between Member States of the Community on the procurement and manufacture of defence equipment is not the result of any coherent, long-term policy, but relates solely to isolated projects, where the partners have usually had to choose between collaboration or abandonment of the project, the logical consequence of which is to buy American equipment.

2. The Negative Effects of the EEC Member States' Present Policy on Procurement

The problems associated with the attainment of interoperability and standardisation of the various types of defence equipment used in Western

Europe have been discussed virtually ever since NATO was established in 1949, both within NATO and in other bodies set up for purposes of cooperation in the field of defence policy. A characteristic feature of these discussions has been the broad measure of agreement both on the desirability of attaining interoperability and some degree of standardisation and on increased industrial cooperation in Western Europe as being the best way of meeting these objectives. At the same time, however, the progress made so far stands in glaring contrast to this agreement in principle.

The modest results so far obtained may be due to the fact that, at least until recently, the problem has largely been regarded as a question of military efficiency seen in relation to the size of defence budgets, whereas a secondary rôle has been accorded in the general discussion to the aspects relating to industrial policy.

Military experts have confirmed that the attainment of interoperability of defence equipment was to be regarded as an absolute minimum requirement and that standardisation was preferable not only from the point of view of the cost, but also from that of the efficiency of logistic support. Non-standardised but interoperable equipment could not, in the event of damage, be repaired and supplied with new spare parts in allied countries using different types of weapons, unless these countries held special stocks of spare parts, special tools for such equipment and, in many cases, had specially trained personnel too. Interoperable but non-standardised equipment would therefore far more rapidly become unusable as a result of minor damage in situations where equipment was dependent on an allied country's supply and maintenance facilities.

From the industry's point of view the interoperability issue is of little or no relevance: it may mean that certain modifications in equipment specifications will have to be made, but apart from this, the achievement of interoperability will hardly have any effect on the conditions under which

European armaments industry is working today.

Standardisation on the other hand is strongly linked with the problem of restructuring and rationalising armaments production in Europe. It is hard to see how any kind of large-scale production could be established, be it in the form of licence-production, co-production or division of labour between national industries without standardisation of the equipment concerned.

A characteristic feature of the discussions to date has been the predominant concern with industry as a means for achieving specific defence policy objectives. The pursuit of specifically industrial objectives in the context of a common policy for the manufacture and procurement of defence equipment has not, on the other hand, occupied a particularly prominent place in the general discussion. The reason for this is to be sought in the fact that, up to now, discussion of these problems has taken place within organisations chiefly concerned with defence policy, viz. NATO, Western European Union, FINABEL and, most recently, IEPG.

Greater attention than has been the case hitherto should be given to the industrial arguments in these discussions.

It is well-known, for example, that the large sums spent in the USA on intensified research and development into military aircraft technology have played a vital part in giving American aircraft manufacturers the leading position they today occupy in European civil aircraft markets, because civil aircraft manufacturers have been able to take over the research findings of the military branch of the industry virtually free of charge. For example, the development in the early 1950s of American long-distance bombers formed the technological basis for the first generation of American jet passenger aircraft. This lead, the foundations of which were laid in the early 1960s, is still being increased with, in value terms, civil aircraft constructed in the EEC obtaining only a 21.2% share of the Community market in 1976. The remainder went more or less entirely to American manufacturers.

For military aircraft, the situation is somewhat better: in 1975 military aircraft manufactured in the Community accounted in value terms for 67% of the EEC Member States' total military fleet.

The combination of less resources for military research and development in the European aircraft industry and the dispersal of these resources between a far larger number of companies has undoubtedly had an extremely adverse effect on the competitiveness of the military and civil sector.

Another adverse effect of uncoordinated purchases of military hardware distributed over a wide range of types of equipment and hence leading to production on a smaller scale is that this practice is helping to maintain the existing manufacturing structure in the aviation industry. The characteristic feature of this production structure is that a far larger number of companies than in the USA (1975: 19 in the Community as against 8 in the USA) have to share a substantially lower turnover (1975: 7.4 billion units of account[1] in the Community as against 17.6 billion units of account in the USA). This means that both the military and civil aviation industries in Western Europe are badly placed from the competitive point of view: their research and development activities overlap, the effectiveness of these activities is reduced and the cost of their products is pushed up disproportionately while, at the same time, the financial benefits of economies of scale cannot be exploited. The result is that not only civil aircraft production in Western Europe but to an increasing extent the military branch of the industry too is threatened by a severe cutback, unless military procurement policy is used as a means for promoting increased collaboration across national frontiers in the field of production.

The difficult situation in which the European data-processing industry currently finds itself can

---

[1] A standard way of equating expenditure used in the European Community. 1 unit of account = £0.65 (October 1978).

also to some extent be attributed to an official procurement policy, in both the military and civil sectors, aimed above all at serving short-term national interests in the field of industry policy. In view of the growing importance of the military sector as a customer for the most advanced technology in this field, future efforts to improve the situation by coordinating the procedures for the award of public supply contracts[1] in the civil sector will scarcely have the desired effect on industrial policy, unless a similar policy is adopted for the military sector.

Another industry of rapidly growing importance for the military sector is the electronics industry. Unlike the aircraft and data-processing industries the electronics industry cannot at present be said to be in a crisis, although it is faced with increasing competition from Japan, the USA and other third countries. The lack of a coordinated military procurement policy acting as an industrial incentive particularly as regards research and development, may in the long term make the European electronics industry less competitive in relation to countries where this industry has the support of such a policy.

The shipyards of the Member States to a large extent depend on the construction of warships, an activity which, in the present state of crisis, can be essential for the survival of a shipyard. Also in this field great advantage could be gained through a restructuring which should result in the individual countries and shipyards concentrating their efforts on the construction of the types of ships where they had the highest degree of expertise. Military experts have informed the committee of cases where there was a difference in price of more than 100% of warships with the same combat efficiency, produced in two different EEC Member States.

Similar considerations apply to the equipment of

---

[1] The Council Directive of 21 December 1976 on coordinating procedures for the award of public supply contracts excluded the data-processing sector from its field of application, provisionally until 1981.

the ships which accounts for a steadily increasing part of the total production costs and which to a considerable extent is produced by other branches of industry, as, for example, the electronics industry.

Lastly, mention can be made of the predominantly military industries that are engaged in the manufacture of lightly and heavily armed armoured vehicles, various kinds of artillery, hand weapons and ammunition. Several of these industries can at present be described as relatively competitive. For these industries, the chief effect of a policy of cooperation with regard to the procurement of military equipment that was geared to industrial objectives, would therefore be to consolidate the position of competitive undertakings and, in the longer term, to improve conditions for a number of those companies at present under threat of closure.

Generally speaking, it has to be said of the Member States' defence equipment industry that its output falls considerably short of what could be achieved by the Member States pursuing a broader orientated weapons procurement policy, speaking in terms of time as well as geography.

Firstly, coordinated production would immediately make it possible to deliver more equipment to the participating states within the same budgetary limits thanks to the economy of scale which would be obtained.

In addition, the products in question would at the same time become more competitive in both existing and potential export markets, especially the USA, with the result that there could very well be a substantial rise in the industry's total turnover.

The adverse effects of the individual Community countries' present policies on defence procurement cannot unfortunately be said to be limited to the defence material industry as such. Current overlapping in the field of research and development means that the results of these activities are inferior to what could be obtained by a coordinated effort or, alternatively, taking existing research findings as our criterion, these findings could have been obtained with a far smaller effort and resources could have been released for research and development in civil sectors. In both cases, the result would be that the general level of research and technology would be higher than is the case at present.

It is difficult to quantify in precise terms the financial loss due to overlapping research and development activities. Seen in the Atlantic context (the European NATO countries plus the USA) Thomas A. Callaghan Jr. estimates that the US $ 2,600 million (the figure for 1974-1975) expended annually on research and development in Western Europe are an outright waste, arguing that these areas are already covered by the US $ 7,600 million spent by the USA on similar activities. Even though this estimate is probably exaggerated, it nevertheless gives some indication of the magnitude of the wastage that is taking place.

There is no evidence to suggest that the overlap in the field of research and development between the Western European countries internally is any less than that between these countries and the USA. Just one look at the multiplicity of types of weapons with the same functions in use with the armed forces of the Western European countries should be sufficient to give an indication of the extent of this waste.

The loss to society resulting from the present policy is also reflected in the fact that, if defence budgets are taken as the yardstick, individual countries are getting far too little defence for their money or, if their existing defence capability is taken as the yardstick, are paying far too much for what they are getting.[1]

---

[1] For the sake of accuracy it should be noted that, in computing the total wastage resulting from the present policy, the increased purchase costs to the countries concerned cannot be aggregated with previous wastage at the R&D and manufacturing stages. The additional cost at the purchasing stage represents society's payment for the wastage that has already occurred and is not therefore in itself wastage.

The waste of resources set aside for defence purposes does not, however, stop with the procurement of non-standardised equipment manufactured on a small scale. The training of operating and maintenance personnel and the setting up of repair and maintenance facilities will, as a rule, be far more expensive for equipment of this nature.

It is difficult to quantify the waste involved here, but a figure that suggests itself is something at least of the same order of magnitude as that identified at the procurement stage.

All in all it has to be said therefore that the Community countries' present policy with regard to the procurement of defence equipment entails an unwarrantable waste of economic resources which, whether seen in the light of a given defence capability or a given defence budget, is detrimental to the national economy as a whole as well as to employment.

3. Possible Forms of Cooperation between Industry, the Procurement Authorities and Firms

The committee has no wish to pick out any one form of cooperation as being preferable to any other, as the choice between the various alternatives will depend very much on the actual circumstances under which cooperation is to take place. It will therefore confine itself to a brief survey of the major forms of cooperation, together with some of the advantages and disadvantages attributed to them by the experts.

A. Research and development phase

The R&D phase would normally be the responsibility of one firm, the project leader, possibly with other firms as sub-contractors for parts of the project. 'Decentralised' R&D, where several firms work in parallel on different parts of a single project, is a rarity in practice and is regarded by the experts as undesirable. Therefore there does not seem to be a great deal of choice at this stage when it comes to forms of industrial cooperation.

Further, the R&D phase would normally take one of the following two forms, or a variant thereof:

No special planning or financing of R&D by the procurement bodies
Advantages: Initially, savings by the procurement authorities. May also encourage competition.
Disadvantages: The necessary R&D may not be carried out so that no usable systems can be offered to the procurement authorities, which are then forced to purchase elsewhere. Risk of overlapping R&D efforts. Moreover, R&D costs will frequently be added to the price of the complete system, so that savings achieved at the earlier stage disappear.

There is a risk that production capacity will gradually cease to exist.

R&D planned in cooperation with the procurement authority, and financed wholly or in part by the latter
Advantages: R&D geared to the customers' needs, and overlapping largely avoided. A high level of technology can be maintained, together with future production capacity, also in those firms whose R&D contracts do not perhaps lead directly to production contracts.
Disadvantages: Initially, higher cost to the procurement authorities. This cost may increase still further if, to ensure competition, there is 'planned overlapping' i.e. if identical R&D contracts are placed with several firms, only one of which will probably obtain a production contract.

B. Production phase

One major restriction on the choice of the form of cooperation is the fact that the R&D phase must in large part be planned to fit in with the production facilities actually available. Changes here, for example, by the enlistment of new production partners, may therefore entail the need to alter the original project, with consequent delays and cost increases. It is therefore vital to decide on subsequent production structure at the R&D stage. Within these limits, the following forms of cooperation are possible:

Large-scale nationally based production, as part of an international division of labour and consequently designed wholly or partially to meet all participants' needs in the sector

Advantages: Civil and military experts regard a division of labour on these lines, with production taking place where there is greatest expertise, as the ideal form of cooperation. It would provide the best weapons systems at the lowest price, as a high level of expertise would be combined with the advantage of long production runs.

Disadvantages: Complete reorganisation of production on these lines is regarded as a pipe-dream by most experts, because of the radical structural changes to the industry that would be required: the less competitive among the participant states would have to take a considerable cut in their armament production, and that would hardly be politically acceptable. This form of cooperation would also involve a high degree of dependence by individual countries on their partners' defence industries, which could scarcely be reconciled with certain countries' aspirations to maintain an independent national defence. Finally, an armaments industry with this degree of specialisation could, under certain circumstance, be more vulnerable to direct military attack or sabotage.

Production under licence
Advantages: Savings on R&D and foreign exchange, if the alternative was to buy equipment abroad. In addition, production under licence automatically provides for standardisation, unless substantial modifications are made to the original design. According to the circumstances, this form of production can be a useful complement in endeavours to apportion production over a longish period of time according to the principle of 'fair returns'.
Disadvantages: If production under licence is dispersed over a number of small production runs, or if substantial design modifications are made (so that in fact production under licence is only partially involved) R&D savings may quickly be wiped out. In extreme cases, equipment built under licence may prove much more expensive than equipment bought from the original manufacturer. Furthermore, production under licence does little to develop domestic R&D capability.

Co-production
This form of cooperation has been more and more widely adopted in recent years.

The Anglo-German-Italian MRCA Tornado project deserves mention as a typical and, to a certain degree, exemplary collaborative effort of this kind. The production side is the responsibility of a joint company, Panavia GmbH[1] while the procurement side is handled by the NATO'S MRCA Management Agency (NAMMA).
Advantages: Collaboration of this kind enables the participating countries to carry out projects which are too ambitious for their individual technological and economic resources. This form of cooperation is also flexible, and can be tailored to meet the requirements of the participants in each individual case. As a rule, both R&D and production costs will be lower per unit produced than they would

---

[1] Partners: Messerschmitt Bölkow-Blohm 42.5%, British Aircraft Corporation 42.5%, Aeritalia 15%.

have been if each participating country had attempted to 'go it alone' – always supposing that such had been feasible in the first place.

Cooperation helps to maintain production capacity and an advanced level of technology in the participating countries. Once it has been established, it may facilitate future collaborative projects and reduce their cost.

Disadvantages: A project organised on these lines will cost more than a similar project carried out on a national basis. Thomas A. Callaghan Jr. estimates that joint production may involve a 20-30% cost increase. However, the alternative he assumes in this calculation, that is to say, nationally based large-scale production as part of an international division of labour must, as has already been said, be qualified as unrealistic in the present European context. If we instead take the realistic alternatives for Europe, that is to say, production under licence, limited national projects with high unit costs, or spending foreign exchange on buying American equipment, the economic disadvantages of joint production are not so easy to demonstrate.

Experience has shown that, if the production and procurement sides are not properly organised, joint projects may be delayed and their costs pushed up as a result of interference by the individual partners' defence ministries, both at the R&D and the production stages.

The lack of continuity of joint production is another disadvantage frequently mentioned. When a project is completed, the project agencies are disbanded and the valuable experience and expertise is lost. However, this could be avoided if the same project agency was given the chance to manage several successive projects.

4. Requirements of a Future Policy on the Procurement and Manufacture

The crucial element here is the definition of military needs and the laying-down on a joint basis of the requirements of the equipment to meet these needs. Here the time factor is extremely important as a period of 8 to 10 years will elapse between the time when the military requirements of, for example, a modern jet aircraft are decided and the first models become operative. Similar time-spans apply to other types of advanced equipment. This means in reality that, if there is to be any hope of seeing the forces in Western Europe even partly equipped with standardised equipment produced in Europe by around 1990 the common military requirements of the various types of equipment must be determined before 1980 and, not long after, a decision must be taken on the approximate numbers the countries in question wish to purchase. Unless action is taken on these lines at an early date to lay down on a joint basis the military requirements for the equipment in question, and this is followed up by cooperation on the manufacture and procurement of standardised material, it is to be feared that the most competitive European undertakings will enter into collaboration on production with American companies and that the remaining European firms will disappear from the market.[1]

The most competitive of the Western European defence equipment manufacturers would undoubtedly regard as sufficient a common procurement policy which meant the drawing-up, within the above time-limits, of common specifications for equipment followed up by options to buy cor-

---

[1] An early indication of just such a trend seems to be provided by the fact that the West German firm Messerschmitt Bölkow-Blohm signed an agreement in the autumn of 1977 with the American company McDonnell-Douglas Corp. on joint studies with a view to the development of a new fighter aircraft.

responding to the anticipated needs of the individual purchasing countries. The industry would then make its own arrangements for cooperation as appropriate, without any intervention on the part of customers.

However, a common policy on this basis alone would not be feasible politically, as it would have a number of unwelcome implications for several of the countries taking part. If a European policy for the procurement and manufacture of defence equipment is to have a chance of gaining general political backing, it must therefore satisfy a number of additional requirements.

The participating states must be provided with guarantees that such cooperation will not have any major adverse effect on their balance of payments by comparison with the existing arrangements. This will not necessarily apply to individual projects but, on the basis of several projects over a number of years, an effort ought to be made to operate the principle of 'juste retour'.

The research findings of a particular project ought to be fully accessible to all undertakings taking part therein. In addition, there is the question whether research findings should also be made available to the participating countries for onward transmission to other undertakings, where undertakings from only some of the countries taking part are involved on the manufacturing side. If this scheme cannot be implemented, steps must be taken to ensure that, over a period of time, projects are allocated in such a way that individual participating countries do not acquire a monopoly of advanced technology in one or more areas.

Indeed, the maintenance of fair competition will be quite a problem in the context of cooperation on the procurement and manufacture of defence equipment. Any long-term compensatory mechanism designed to offset the negative effects on individual countries' balance of payments by according a preferential position to certain manufacturing operations, should not therefore give 100% compensation in the form of preferential orders, but only 75-80% to countries whose industry is less competitive. At the same time, it should be possible for highly competitive countries to obtain a 20-25% balance of payments surplus without this jeopardising their position when future projects are allocated.

Finally, provision ought also to be made for the possibility of cooperation on procurement alone for the purpose of purchasing equipment from third countries. This would be necessary, particularly in the longer term, so as to prevent a few European undertakings from acquiring a virtual monopoly through the restructuring which must take place. Such companies should continue to live with some risk of orders being placed elsewhere.

Cooperation on procurement alone would also be necessary as part of a long-term sharing of work between the USA and Western Europe in the field of defence equipment manufacture. Through close collaboration on procurement, it would be possible to make purchases of American equipment conditional on equivalent purchases by the Americans in Western Europe, hence gradually establishing the much talked-of 'Two-Way Street'.

5. Likely Problems

The problems involved in future cooperation can be divided into purely political problems, and economic, military and technical problems. The first can largely be regarded as a product of the last three problems. The committee would like to emphasise this, since it is generally assumed that the major problems are the political ones. However, this is an optical illusion produced by the circumstance that it is normally the politicians who conduct the final international negotiations, so that opposition which may well originate elsewhere is openly expressed for the first time in political negotiations. In its contacts with national politicians, the committee has been unable to identify any actual political opposition to increased European cooperation in this field, but in some cases a certain degree of confusion in attitudes, or different opinions on the desirable extent of cooperation.

Thus, the restrictions which joint production could impose on certain Member States' arms exports to third countries is primarily an economic problem. Although such cases may also involve certain aspects of foreign policy without any direct economic implications, in most cases the problem would be to compensate the countries in question for lost export opportunities within the framework of the new cooperation arrangements.

The only purely political difficulty encountered was the doctrine in some Member States of maintaining an independent national defence. It must be admitted that this standpoint can create certain, although not insurmountable difficulties, in connection with a reorganisation of the European armaments industry.

The actual economic problems are primarily related to the short-term and narrow economic viewpoints currently governing national procurement policies which again are linked to the short life of most governments calling for results within a short time-span or very firm guarantees for long-term results. The structural changes required to avoid the waste we have demonstrated in the production of defence equipment will mean that some national undertakings will in the short term receive fewer orders than they would obtain under present policies, or must prepare themselves for the difficult process of reorganising their production. It would be unreasonable to expect the industry in any Member State to accept changes of this kind without reasonable guarantees of long-term profit to at least offset the short-term losses. If a proposal for collaboration on defence equipment is to have any real prospects of acceptance it must therefore embody clear guarantees which can be invoked not merely by the participating countries under the principle of fair returns mentioned above, but also by individual undertakings.

The differences in strategic and tactical doctrines which to a certain extent divide the Member States also hamper cooperation, as these differences frequently obstruct the choice of common weapon systems. Here we must distinguish between historically and socially based differences and those based on the different geographical situations.

The Economic Committee feels that the former can best be disposed of by joint studies of long-term trends in military technology and the changes they will probably generate in strategic and tactical doctrines.

However, those caused by geographical factors represent real differences in military requirements, and due attention must be paid to them in the course of future cooperation.

Many technical problems will arise during cooperation between undertakings in different countries. These difficulties, which primarily arise in actual joint manufacture, range from linguistic and legal problems to those originating in differences in technical education, technical language, standards, etc.

Some of these problems can only be overcome by the undertakings themselves in the first stages of cooperation. Experience of joint production ventures shows that this does in fact happen. Considerable extra cost is involved in the early stages, but as the companies get used to cooperation this is rapidly reduced. Calculations of the extra costs involved in joint production, based on the first project carried out by several companies, will therefore often be excessively pessimistic. Many of the difficulties can be avoided if collaboration begins at the R&D stage of a project, as expensive changes to the original design frequently have to be made if the involvement of partners is left until the beginning of production. The draftsman takes the view that joint production is not as expensive as is generally assumed, so long as it is allowed to cover a number of successive projects over a longish time-scale.

The purely legal problems can best be overcome by harmonising the legislation covering both the allocation of research, development and production contracts to the main contractor or contractors, and contracts concluded with sub-suppliers. Changes to company law to facilitate international collaborative production should also be considered.

6. The EEC's Role

The actual decisions on joint weapons procurement are largely based on military considerations, which are outside the competence of the Community and should therefore be entrusted to an institution which is not based on the EEC Treaty, but within which the Communities are adequately represented.

On the other hand, the EEC is the European body best able to organise the restructuring of the European armaments industry, which is vital to the successful introduction of a common procurement policy. Hitherto, the armaments industry in Europe has been a blank spot in Community economic policy, with two unfortunate results: firstly, all attempts to create a common industrial policy have been doomed to failure since they left this sector out, which in 1976 accounted for some 22% of all R&D funds in the Community, as against 8% for the improvement of productivity and technology in the rest of industry. Secondly the coordination of procurement and manufacture of weapon systems by the military and defence establishments have in the past resulted merely in a number of fragmented individual projects, because there was no coherent organisation on the production side.

The Community's efforts to achieve an industrial policy should be intensified, and the Member States' defence industries included in those efforts. A new, across-the-board sectoral policy on armaments manufacture should also be introduced to supplement the steps which have already been taken in certain industries (for example, in the aircraft industry and the computer industry) towards a sectoral policy.

In principle there is no difference between an industrial policy for the armaments industry and industrial policy in general, so the committee will refrain from listing all the various instruments of industrial policy; instead it will point to areas where Community intervention would be particularly effective in promoting the requisite restructuring of production in the Community's defence equipment industries.

Legal measures

The elaboration of satisfactory rules to ensure long-term compensation of Member States' industries for the orders which procurement cooperation may initially cause them to lose will prove the most difficult but also the most significant step towards European cooperation on the procurement and manufacturing of defence equipment.

With its experience and skill in trade and industrial policy, the Commission would seem to be the body with the best prospects for putting forward proposals on the subject that will enjoy general support.

The Community could also play an important rôle in improving the legal framework for cooperation between undertakings, both in respect of company law and the law of contract.

Likewise the legal basis for the allocation of R&D contracts and production contracts (including in particular common rules for adjudicating tenders) should, if not actually determined within an EEC framework, be worked out at any rate in collaboration with the Commission.

Financial measures

Another important area where the Community can make itself felt is the financing of industrial R&D, undertaken in cooperation between undertakings in several Member States in areas of special interest to the defence equipment industry but which can improve the competitiveness of non-military industry as well. Most R&D projects in the aircraft industry, the computer industry and the electronics industry fall into this category.

Further the setting up of a common fund to provide resources for structural change in the defence equipment industry would be a natural task for the Community.

Trade and raw materials supply policy

The possibility of using trade policy measures to encourage European manufacturing collaboration should be considered, though the committee is not at present in a position to give an opinion on the advisability of measures of this kind.

Consideration should also be given to the question whether the Communities should not have a part to play in establishing common buffer stocks of strategic raw materials, imported mainly from third countries, so that, in a crisis, production could be maintained in both the defence and civilian industries.

Institutional measures

Further it would in general be desirable for industrial policy to be represented by the Communities in a common European body for the procurement of defence equipment, so that industrial policy aspects might be given due consideration throughout that body's decision-making process.

7. Conclusions

The sharply increasing costs of most types of advanced military equipment, and especially the extremely high research and development costs to be met before production can commence, have brought about a situation where the countries of Europe are more and more frequently confronted with the choice of either manufacturing these types of equipment in cooperation, or buying them from third countries. Where the latter solution is adopted, the inevitable result is a reduction, in both quality and quantity, of European defence production capacity, since the technology made available under any offset agreements cannot give industry the same capability as it would acquire in carrying out its own research and development.

In view of the defence industry's role in pioneering new technology, which usually has subsequent civil applications, and since a major part of the industry also manufactures for civil markets, the success or failure of the defence industries will have a marked influence on the competitive position of industry as a whole and consequently on employment.

If we only continue to base defence procurement on what can, in individual cases, be agreed bilaterally or trilaterally, i.e. collaboration on an *ad hoc* basis, without an integrated, structured European defence material industry and market, we are risking, in the worst case, a serious decline in the Western European defence industry and, at the very least, throwing away the opportunity of improving the quality and output of the industry by the rational use of available resources.

In the light of the above, any further attempts to establish a common industrial policy which does not include this key sector would be indefensible. On the other hand, the inclusion of the defence industries in a future Community industrial policy calls for simultaneous progress by Member States on those aspects of defence equipment policy not covered by the EEC Treaty.

As a first step discussions must therefore be initiated by the Commission to define each side's potential responsibilities concerning the development of a common armaments procurement policy within the overall framework of a common industrial policy. When this has been done, the Commission should put forward an action programme as outlined in this report, representing the industrial policy aspect which has been missing in previous attempts to reorganise the European defence equipment market.

Part III
THE RESOLUTION of the European Parliament on European armaments procurement adopted at Strasbourg on 14 June 1978

The European Parliament

– having regard to its resolution of 15 December 1975 on the effects of a European foreign policy on defence questions:
– having regard to the proposal made by Mr Tindemans in his report to the European Council on European Union that the establishment of a European Armaments Agency should be considered:
– having regard to the draft resolution drawn up by the representatives of the Member States of the European Economic Community, meeting within the Council, relating to the purchase and development of aircraft weapon systems, appended to the Action Programme for the European Aeronautical Sector submitted by the Commission to the Council on 3 October 1975:
– having regard to its resolution of 6 July 1976 on the report and proposals from the Commission to the Council on the European aeronautical sector:
– considering that the establishment of a jointly organised European armaments industry with a structured market is an essential element in

THE RESOLUTION

developing a common industrial policy:
– considering that the civil and defence aspects of certain key industries, such as the construction of air-frames and missiles, air engines, ship-building and electronics, cannot be separated in planning their future development:
– considering the need for European industry to remain technologically up-to-date and competitive:
– having regard to the report of the Political Affairs Committee and the opinion of the Committee on Economic and Monetary Affairs
– considering the need to achieve a better balance between United States arms sales to Europe and European arms sales to the United States:
1. Calls on the Commission to submit to the Council in the near future a European action programme for the development and production of conventional armaments within the framework of the common industrial policy:
2. Instructs its President to forward this resolution and the report of its committee to the Council and the Commission, the Foreign Ministers meeting in political cooperation and the Governments and Parliaments of the Member States.

Part IV
Data

1. Examples of European and Atlantic Procurement Cooperation

A. European

In his study 'Weapons procurement in Europe – capabilities and choices' Roger Facer lists the main current European collaborative procurement projects. Since definitions of 'collaborative procurement' vary, this summary covers projects in which two or more countries have collaborated in the design of major systems, generally sharing management responsibility. It excludes licensed production and projects which involve only multinational sub-contracting for production for one country within another.

The aircraft sector is the most important. The major current project is the Multi-Rôle Combat Aircraft (MRCA). The MRCA is being developed by Britain, Germany and Italy. It is a supersonic variable-geometry aircraft, designed to meet the three differing sets of requirements of the three countries concerned.

The MRCA is administered by the NATO MRCA Management Agency (NAMMA), which is answerable to the participating countries through the NATO MRCA Management Organisation (NAMMO). The airframe is being built by Panavia with participation by the British Aircraft Corporation, Messerschmitt-Bölkow-Blohm and Aeritalia. The engine is being built by Turbo-Union, in which Rolls Royce, Motoren und Turbinen Union (MTU) and Fiat participate. A company called Avionica Systems Engineering (ASE) has been established to carry out the project planning of the avionics and coordinate the work of the avionics contractors.

The Jaguar has been developed by Britain and France. It is a supersonic strike and trainer aircraft, based on a Bréguet design. Production is supervised by the intergovernmental Jaguar Committee. The construction is divided equally between British Aircraft Corporation and Dassault-Bréguet for the airframe and equally between Rolls Royce and Turbomeca for the engine.

The Franco-German supersonic ground-attack/trainer, Alpha Jet, is being developed and built jointly by Dassault-Bréguet and Dornier. It will be powered by SNECMA/Turbomeca engines.

The Belgian-French-German C-160 medium-range military transport aircraft was developed and built by SNECMA (with Rolls Royce engines built under licence) in France, and by MTU in Germany, and Fabrique Nationale d'Armes de Guerre in Belgium.

The Bréguet Atlantique maritime-patrol aircraft was a NATO project, which produced aircraft for France, Germany, Italy and the Netherlands. It was developed and built by a consortium called Societé Européene pour la Construction de Bréguet Atlantique formed by Dornier (Germany), ABAP (Belgium), Fokker-VFW (Netherlands), Bréguet and Aérospatiale (France), later joined by Aeritalia (Italy).

Another development has been that of the Puma/Gazelle/Lynx helicopters between Britain and France. These helicopters have been developed by Westland and Aérospatiale.

There have also been a number of effective cooperative projects in the field of missiles; thus a number of British and French firms have joined together to produce the Martel Anglo-French air-to-surface guided missile. A ship-launched surface-to-surface version has also been developed.

France and Germany have developed, jointly, a low-level surface-to-air guided weapon, Roland, and the high-speed anti-tank wire-guided missiles,

MILAN and HOT.

French and German firms have collaborated in the development and production of the long-range air-to-ship missile, the KORMORAN.

The Franco-Italian OTOMAT surface-to-surface naval missile has been developed, and an air-launched version for maritime patrol aircraft, ALBATROS, is following.

British and Belgian firms have been cooperating in developing the · Atlas lightweight anti-tank missile.

Britain and Germany have cooperated with Canada in developing the CL-89 (AN/USD-501) short-range reconnaissance drone.

Also, Britain, Germany and Italy are cooperating in the development of the FH-70, 155mm towed gun and its associated ammunition. A self-propelled version is also being developed.

Belgium and Britain have been developing a combat reconnaissance vehicle programme for the development and production of a family of light aluminium air-portable vehicles. This family of vehicles already includes the Scorpion light tank and the Striker, which carried a long-range anti-tank missile.

B. ATLANTIC

At the Atlantic level, the Assistant Secretary-General of NATO for Defence Support, Mr Walter LaBerge, lists, based on information supplied by Admiral Kidd, the Supreme Allied Commander Atlantic, in the December 1976 issue of 'Nato Review', a number of 'collaborative efforts by NATO nations in naval armaments that have been successful'. The list sets out: NATO MK 44 torpedo; NATO MPA aircraft (Atlantic); NATO Azores fixed acoustic range (AFAR); NATO acoustic communication with submarines; NATO Sea Sparrow; NATO helicopters, Lynx, Puma and

Gazelle; NATO patrol craft hydrofoil missile (PHM); NATO naval forces sensor and weapon accuracy check sites (FORACS); NATO frigate for the 1970's; NATO Sea Gnat system; NATO conventionally powered submarine for employment in European waters.

The following projects are listed, also in the field of naval armaments, as having 'the potential for success':

Very short range air defence weapon system; explosion resistant multi-influence, sweep system for mines (ERMISS), electro-optical devices; NATO anti-surface ship missile (ASSM); NATO small surface-to-air ship self-defence system for the post 1985 time frame (NATO '6S' system).

'Other collaborative efforts by NATO nations that have been successful in areas other than naval armaments' are listed as follows:

F104G Starfighter; Fiat G91 strike fighter; Hawk missile; Sidewinder missile; Bull-pup missile; AS-30 Missile; Jaguar tactical and training aircraft; multi-rôle combat aircraft (MRCA); NADGE air defence system (80 sites); NATO multi-national F-16 air combat fighter; 220 NATO airfields with common communications and pipeline links for support; 28 allied tactical publications (ATP's) containing common doctrine; 53 allied communications publications (ACP's) containing common communications procedures and doctrine; nearly 900 standardisation agreements have been made between NATO nations to enable their forces to operate together in the most effective manner.

A number of the above projects have already been referred to in the earlier list of examples of cooperation at the European level.

A number of other projects, either bilateral or multi-lateral, between members of the Alliance that have been 'beneficial in achieving greater standardisation', include:

Harpoon missile; 3 inch/76 millimetre OTO Melara gun; Terrier missile; Olympus/Tyne engines; M20 series fire control systems; Tri-partite mine counter-measures; (MCM) vessel; Exocet missile.

> Finally, Mr LaBerge sets out his view that NATO could 'improve its degree of standardisation or interoperability in the following areas':
> 41 different types of naval guns from 20 mm upwards; 31 different types of anti-tank weapons; 6 different types of recoilless rifle; 36 different types of fire control radars; 8 different SAM systems; 6 different types of anti-surface ship missiles (ASSM's); common identification system (IFF); common data link; nations' implementation of standardisation agreements (STANAGS); NATO RD & P programmes; nations to harmonise national armament schedules; Establish Test and Evaluation programme; integrate RD & P of armaments into defence planning process.

2. Which is the Appropriate Institution? – supplementary comments by Dr Egon Klepsch

Two distinct points seem to be involved. First, whether NATO, WEU, the Eurogroup or any other body is more appropriate than the European Community to develop European armaments procurement cooperation. Second, whether the European Community is at present or might be, in the future, an appropriate body to achieve such cooperation.

(a) The Atlantic Alliance

The North Atlantic Treaty itself does not make specific reference to armaments production. The nearest it comes to doing so is in Article 3 of the Treaty which states that: 'In order more effectively to achieve the objectives of this Treaty, the Parties, separately and jointly, by means of continuous and effective self-help and mutual aid will maintain and develop their individual and collective capacity to resist armed attack.'

However, the Member Governments of the Atlantic Alliance always interpret the Atlantic Treaty in a very wide sense and they have frequently taken decisions on the basis of common accord between themselves rather than that of a legal text. Thus the decisions taken within the Alliance to establish bodies such as the Conference of National Armaments Directors (CNAD), the Military Agency for Standardisation (MAS) or the NATO Industrial Advisory Group (NIAG) have been taken by the parties concerned on a pragmatic rather than juridical basis. The pragmatic basis of Alliance activities concerning procurement cooperation in no way lessens or detracts from the competences of the Alliance to work in this area.

There seem to be two distinct reasons why the Atlantic Alliance would not be a suitable institution to develop *European* procurement cooperation. The first reason is that the Atlantic Alliance is an Atlantic and not a European Institution. Thus, the United States and Canada are just as concerned in procurement cooperation within the Alliance as any European State. This means that at any stage the United States could use its very strong influence against the development or the choice of a European weapons system or armaments project if it were in competition with an American one. There is a need for rationalisation of weapons production within the Alliance, but if the Europeans are to develop their end of the 'two-way street' they must first of all be able to develop a specifically European procurement system.

Second, although within the Alliance, specialised groups such as CNAD and NIAG have a very high degree of military and technical expertise they do not have the competences and the ability to structure and organise – at the level of the European Community – a single market in armaments. Only the Community, within the framework of a common industrial policy, and through action taken by the Commission, if so empowered by the Council, could do this.

(b) Western European Union (WEU)

In theory WEU should provide an admirable forum for armaments procurement cooperation. First, Article 5 of the modified Brussels Treaty linking the members of WEU together, sets out an automatic commitment to mutual defence which goes further than the comparable article of the North Atlantic Treaty. Second, France has been, from the very beginning, a full member of WEU, whereas although it is a member of the Atlantic Alliance and takes a full part in the political work of the Alliance, it does not take part in the integrated military structure of NATO.

But although a Standing Armaments Committee was set up in 1955 in order to encourage the development of cooperation in armaments production in WEU, there has been more talk than action concerning procurement cooperation. As early as 1958, the Standing Armaments Committee itself found that 'there is little chance at aiming at efficacious production of existing equipment'.[1] Although the Standing Armaments Committee has worked hard on the specification and development of new military equipment, practical results of this work have been extremely limited. Furthermore, the diminishing political rôle enjoyed by WEU in general has inevitably affected, in an adverse sense, its potential concerning the development of effective measures of procurement cooperation. The discriminations against Germany and in favour of the United Kingdom which are built into the modified Brussels Treaty also adversely influence the possibilities of a dramatic reinvigoration of the work of this institution. It should also be noted that Western European Union has no Treaty-based competences to organise industrial or commercial aspects of the armaments industry.

WEU itself does not view its future in quite the same way. Thus the report recently submitted to the WEU Assembly by Mr Forni, as rapporteur of

---

[1] Third Report of the Council to the Assembly of WEU.

the General Affairs Committee of the Assembly, and dated 4 November 1977 argues that the decision taken by the Council of WEU in May 1976 asking the Standing Armaments Committee to carry out a study of the armaments industries in the WEU Member States, opens up a new rôle for the Standing Armaments Committee.

Mr Forni states 'Until the enquiries conducted by the SAC have led to a published report, it is difficult to say what this rôle will be. But it can already be foreseen that one of its aims will be to remove the obstacles to dividing work between European industries rationally enough to allow worthwhile reductions in the cost price of armaments by lowering operational and marketing expenses as well as investments, without Europe's defence potential suffering. Secondly, a remedy will have to be found for the difficulties to which the European industries are subjected because the crisis in the capitalist world favours large non-European manufacturers.'

Mr Forni's report holds that the Standing Armaments Committee might also 'consider the overall problem of arms sales with a view to reaching a common definition of principles seeking to reduce the scale of arms sales and prevent them from upsetting the balance and fanning the flames of conflicts outside Europe.'

Mr Forni proposes that the Standing Armaments Committee might create 'a European office for the armaments trade to harmonise principles and practice in selling countries with a view to preventing unrestrained competition leading to the over-arming of countries whose only real priority should be economic development.'

Mr Forni concludes his arguments by claiming that the mandate of the Standing Armaments Committee is 'economic rather than military'. He states that whereas the military aspect should be left to the IEPG and that the economic role of the Standing Armaments Committee 'should eventually place it in the framework of the future European Union rather than NATO, making it something of an extension of the Community institutions to the armaments field.'

It is unrealistic to think in terms of the development of WEU and its Standing Armaments Committee into an effective means of structuring and organising the European armaments industry. This aim could best be achieved within the context of a common industrial policy and following initiatives taken by the Commission of the European Community, a mandate given to it by the Council of the Community.

The conclusions arrived at by Mr Forni himself indicate that even in WEU it is realised that the Community framework is a more appropriate one than that of WEU itself in organising the industrial and commercial aspects of the European armaments industry. Further, it seems unlikely that the Member Governments of WEU, all of which are members of the Community, would give a mandate to the WEU Standing Armaments Committee to carry out a mission which is essentially one of promoting the Community's common industrial policy.

The military requirements of new armaments should be defined by the IEPG, and there should be close cooperation between the Community and the IEPG in this respect.

(c) FINABEL

FINABEL's rôle, although an extremely useful one, is essentially that of encouraging background cooperation and studies between its participating States concerning certain aspects of land armaments.

In view of the very limited and technical nature of FINABEL's work, which is, in any case, carried on solely between military staffs, it is inconceivable that FINABEL could be given, let alone carry through, a mandate to develop, at the industrial level, effective armaments procurement cooperation.

(d) EURONAD

For most practical purposes, Euronad has now been replaced by the IEPG, on which all the participating Governments now place the main emphasis. Thus, despite two residual functions still retained by Euronad it seems more relevant to examine the competences of the IEPG concerning procurement cooperation.

(e) The Independent European Programme Group (IEPG)

It has already been stressed that there is outstanding importance in the work of IEPG and, especially, its considerable potential concerning the development of European armaments procurement cooperation.

Conclusions

The conclusions and proposals set out together with the suggested institutional structure of a European armaments procurement agency are based on the assumption that it is the IEPG which is the most effective and most suitable body now working in the procurement field. But, as has been stressed, one of the main reasons that has prevented the development of closer procurement cooperation has been the fact that the military/political institutions engaged in arms procurement (i.e. NATO and its specialised agencies, and WEU, FINABEL, EURONAD and the IEPG) have lacked the potential capability of the European Community to organise the industrial side of arms procurement or to create a structured common Western European armaments market.

It is essentially through close cooperation between the Commission of the European Community on the one hand, and the IEPG on the other, that some form of 'European armaments procurement agency' could most effectively be constructed and that efficient European armaments procurement cooperation could be achieved.

3. Defence-related Industries – Defence Output[1] and Defence Share of Total Output

Industry	Britain (1968)[2] Defence output	% of total output	France (1969)[3] Defence output	% of total output	Germany (1969)[4] Defence output	% of total output
Airframes and missiles	815	52.9	540	46	175	70-80
Aero-engine					100	
Shipbuilding	396	34.3	18	4	72	5-10
Motor Vehicles	104	2.1	72	1.2	140	5-10
Ammunition and explosives	246	2.9	45	40	100	'depends heavily'
Engineering and ordnance			117	7	222	5-10
Electronics	600	9.1	396	45	317	5-10

(From 'Weapons Procurement in Europe – Capabilities and Choices' by Roger Facer, IISS, London 1975)

[1] In $ million; taking $1 = £0.417, 5.55fr, DM4.
[2] Proportion of gross output generated by defence demand, as calculated by Roy Morris in 'The Industrial Impact of Defence Expenditure, 1963 and 1968 – An Input-Output Study' (unpublished paper). The shipbuilding figures include ship repairing and the Royal Dockyards.
[3] Source: Jean Blancard, 'Conception et Réalisation des Armements', in 'Revue de Défense Nationale', February 1971. The shipbuilding and ammunition and explosives figures exclude the activities of the relevant 'Directions Techniques'.
[4] Source: 'White Paper 1970 on the Security of the Federal Republic of Germany and on the State of the Federal German Armed Forces' (Bonn 1970), pp. 147-9. The figures in the right-hand column are not intended to be more precise than the general statements in the text of this source.

4. POSSIBLE STRUCTURE OF A EUROPEAN ARMAMENTS PROCUREMENT AGENCY AS PROPOSED BY DR EGON KLEPSCH

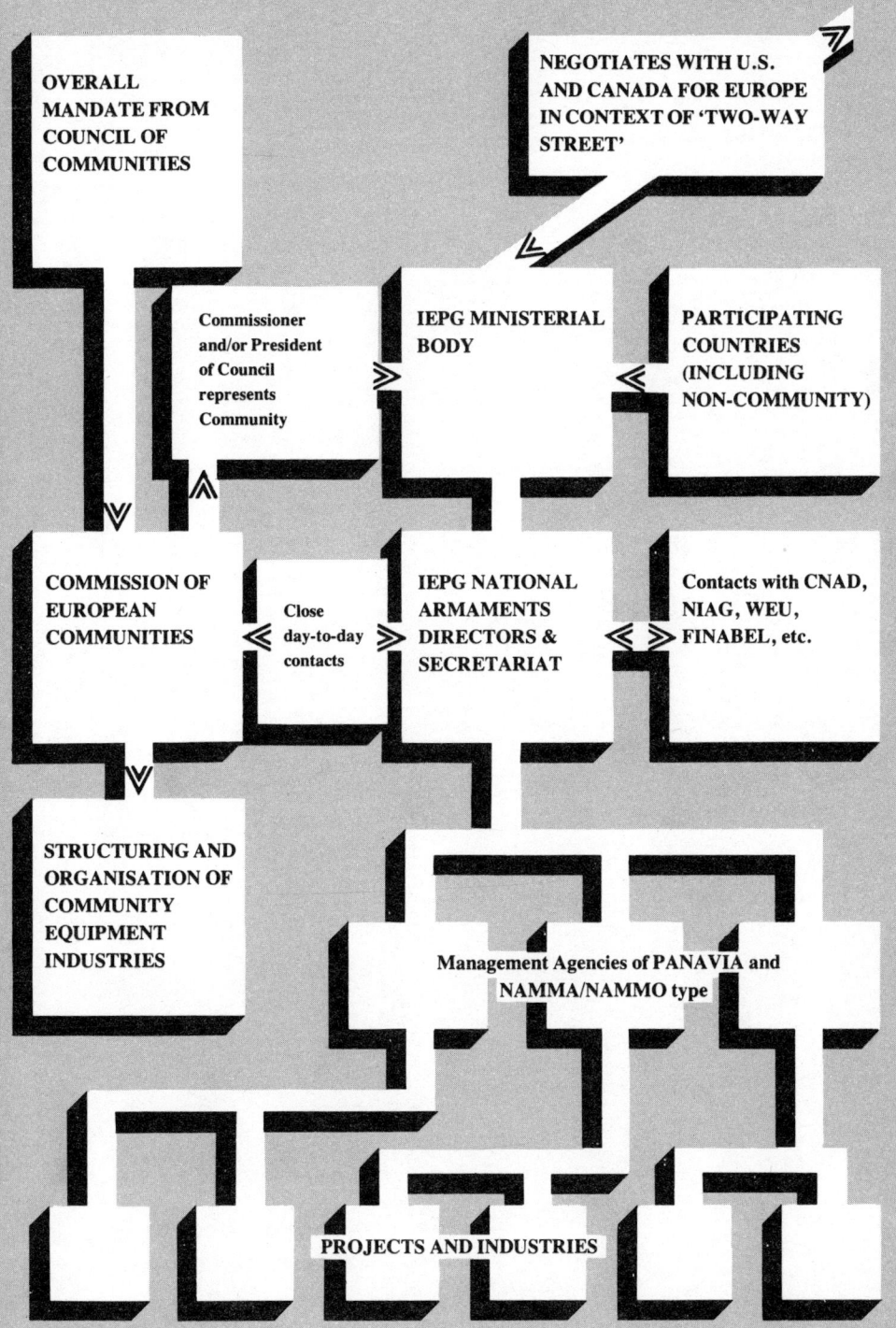